Federal Fumbles:
100 Ways the Government Dropped the Ball

United States Government
US Senate

Senator James Lankford

My fellow taxpayers:

Welcome to the first annual release of the *Federal Fumbles* report! Our national debt is careening toward $19 trillion (yes, that is a *19* followed by 12 zeros), and federal regulations are expanding at a record pace. Meanwhile families struggle to get home loans, and small businesses struggle to make ends meet. States are constantly handed unfunded mandates and executive fiats that they are forced to implement with minimal direction and no way to pay for them. I present this report as a demonstration of ways we can cut back on wasteful federal spending and burdensome regulations to help families, small businesses, and our economy begin to get out from under the weight of federal stagnation.

Cited here are not only prime examples of wasteful spending, but also federal departments or agencies that regulate outside the scope of the federal government's constitutional role. I firmly believe my staff and I have the obligation to solve the troubles of our nation, not just complain, which is why for every problem identified, you will also find a recommended solution. There is a way to eliminate wasteful, ineffective, or duplicative program spending; develop oversight methods to prevent future waste; and find ways to get us back on track.

Over the years other Members of Congress, including former Senator Tom Coburn, current Senators Dan Coats, Jeff Flake, John McCain, Rand Paul, Rep. Steve Russell, along with the House Republican Study Committee, have offered ideas to eliminate wasteful spending. It takes countless months, days, and hours to go through agency budgets, GAO reports, and Inspectors General reviews to identify, research, and fact-check government waste. It should not be this difficult to find out how exactly our government spends money. Federal spending information should not be limited to Members of Congress and their staffs. So here is one solution: the Taxpayer's Right to Know Act.

In January I introduced the Taxpayer's Right to Know Act, which creates a central database for the financial data of every federal program in all federal agencies and departments. Agencies and departments would be required to develop performance metrics for all of their programs and provide a yearly report card. This centralized database would provide an accessible source for everyone to see how our federal government spends money and how effectively that money is used. You have every right to know how your government spends your money. Sunlight is the solution to most of our federal waste.

It is important to remember that while wasteful government spending is harmful, overly burdensome federal regulations are an equal part of the problem facing American families and businesses. The federal government diligently tracks total tax collections and annual spending levels. However, it does not officially account for total government-wide regulatory costs. While certain regulations are important to keep us safe, the current Administration has churned out new regulations at a pace that exceeds 3,500 per year.

To put that into perspective, last year, the President signed 224 bills into law but published 3,554 final rules. This means that for every law passed by Congress, the federal government created 16 new rules. These 3,554 regulations impose significant costs on the American economy. The National Association of Manufacturers calculated the total cost of federal regulations in 2012 to be a staggering $2.028 trillion (11 percent of the U.S. gross domestic product). If our $2 trillion federal regulatory cost were a country, it would be the ninth-largest in the world.

The federal government collected $1.234 trillion in individual income taxes in 2013 but cost individuals and businesses more than $2 trillion in federal regulations. In 2014 the federal government published 80 "major" final regulations that were "economically significant," or regulations that "will cost more than $100 million a year." And remember, the costs of those regulations are passed on to you, the consumer.

Here is a fun fact: last year, according to the Competitive Enterprise Institute, families spent $14,974 of their average household income on goods and services to cover the cost of federal regulations. Can you imagine what your family could do with an additional $14,974 for groceries, gasoline, and savings? Congress owes it to the American people to carefully scrutinize the regulatory process to ensure regulations work for the people. We can balance responsible regulations with cost-effective solutions that work for families. If we do not stop the rising tide of excessive federal regulations, how will the next generation of leaders start the next great American company or afford basic expenses for the family?

I am a proud father of two wonderful girls. I believe there are endless possibilities for the young people of today, as they prepare to be the leaders of tomorrow. My primary mission in the U.S. Senate is to leave the next generation a nation better off than it is today. That is why I leave my family and my home in Oklahoma to come to Washington, DC, each week. I want our government to provide its necessary and essential services and protections—no more, no less. I do not want the federal government to burden our society with its overregulation and overwhelming debt.

It is time for all elected officials in the Senate, House of Representatives, and White House to set priorities, then actually do the work. That is our job. For example, one of our top priorities should be to balance the budget and keep government out of the daily lives of American citizens. An unnecessary challenge is that we often cannot find the common ground to even set priorities, much less decide how to accomplish them. We can all agree that the federal government has a job to do. It is time for us to pick up the ball, and do the work our constituents sent us here to do.

I hope this book provides practical ideas for my fellow Members of Congress, their staffs, and individuals throughout government who can play a role to eliminate careless federal spending and burdensome regulations.

In God We Trust,

James Lankford
United States Senator for Oklahoma

To read more on the Taxpayer's Right to Know Act, please click here.

To go further in-depth on the cost and size of federal regulations, please visit:
Federal Register: Public Law Numbers
CRS Report: Counting Regulations: An Overview of Rulemaking, Types of Federal Regulations, and Pages in the Federal Register
National Association of Manufacturers: The Cost of Federal Regulation to the U.S. Economy, Manufacturing and Small Business
Competitive Enterprise Institute: Ten Thousand Commandments: An Annual Snapshot of the Federal Regulatory State

KEY

As you read through this book you will notice each entry starts with a short "Quick Stats" section that lists the Conference, Team, Fumble, and How to Recover the Ball. The Conference is either Spending or Regulation to tell you whether the entry is an example of wasteful or duplicative spending or a burdensome regulation. The federal agency or department responsible for the problem highlighted is the Team. The cost of the spending or regulation is the Fumble. How to Recover the Ball is a proposed solution to either prevent the Fumble from happening again or stop a regulation from burdening American families and businesses.

ABBREVIATIONS

Agency for International Development	USAID
Al Qaeda in the Arabian Peninsula	AQAP
Army Corps of Engineers	USACE
Bureau of Indian Affairs	BIA
Bureau of Indian Education	BIE
Bureau of Land Management	BLM
California Gnatcatcher	CAGN
Centers for Medicare and Medicaid Services	CMS
Compressed Natural Gas	CNG
Congressional Budget Office	CBO
Crime Victims Fund	CVF
Democratic Republic of the Congo	DRC
Department of Agriculture	USDA
Department of Commerce	DOC
Department of Defense	DOD
Department of Education	DOEd
Department of Energy	DOE
Department of Health and Human Services	HHS
Department of Homeland Security	DHS
Department of Housing and Urban Development	HUD
Department of Justice	DOJ
Department of Labor	DOL
Department of State	State
Department of the Interior	DOI
Department of Transportation	DOT
Department of the Treasury	Treasury
Department of Veterans Affairs	VA
Environmental Protection Agency	EPA
Federal Communications Commission	FCC
Federal Highway Administration	FHWA
Federal Protective Service	FPS
Fiscal Year	FY
Fish & Wildlife Service	FWS

Food and Drug Administration	FDA
General Services Administration	GSA
Government Accountability Office	GAO
Immigration and Customs Enforcement	ICE
Inspector General	IG
Internal Revenue Service	IRS
Islamic State of Iraq and the Levant	ISIL
Massachusetts Institute of Technology	MIT
National Cancer Institute	NCI
National Endowment for the Arts	NEA
National Institutes of Health	NIH
National Institute of Standards and Technology	NIST
National Labor Relations Board	NLRB
National Park Service	NPS
National Science Foundation	NSF
Office of Management and Budget	OMB
Renewable Fuel Standard	RFS
Safety & Health Involvement for Truckers	SHIFT
Securities and Exchange Commission	SEC
Social Security Administration	SSA
Social Security Disability Insurance	SSDI
Special Inspector General for Afghanistan Reconstruction	SIGAR
Task Force for Business and Stability Operations	TFBSO
Trade Adjustment Assistance	TAA
Unemployment Insurance	UI
Wild Horses and Burros	WHB

TABLE OF CONTENTS

A $43 Million Gas Station 9
Silent Shakespeare 10
Subsidized Wind 11
A Tale of Woe, ICE Style 12
Federal Student Lunch Standards: The Anti-Popeye 13
Paid Vacation, Federal Style 15
Dishwasher Efficiency Standards 16
Federal Diets 17
Safe Havens for Criminals 18
Got Gnatcatchers? 19
CMS Files Secretive Settlement 20
A $4 Million Rebel 21
Academy Awards Museum Subsidy 22
Russian Cigarettes 23
Toy Guns: Regulatory Hotspot 24
The Truth Is Not Cheap 25
Taxpayer-Funded Media Ethics in India 26
Caution: Read Before Eating! 27
Llamagate 28
Stand-by For Delivery (Maybe) 29
More Money, Fewer Results 30
And While We Are at It… 31
Getting Dressed, *Jetsons* Style 32
No Rocks for Wars 33
Big Billboards, Bigger Regulations 34
Pony Pals: Wild Horses of the Wild West 35
Which Came First, the Chicken or the Egg? 37
Casinos Could Hit Jackpot from Taxpayer-Funded Research 38
Leatherneck Leftovers 39
$30,000 for a Beetle? (Not the Volkswagen Kind) 40
Promises Not Kept 41
All Lit Up! 44
Federal Bike Trails 45
Funding for Phantom Fuels 46
Law vs. Executive Orders 47
Got a Permit for That? 48
USAID: Blame the Afghans, Not Us 49
VA: Return on Solar Investment in just 38.59 Years! 50
Doctor Uncle Sam 51
Lifeline Phone Program 52
Subsidized Sport Stadiums 53
Unfunded Mandates to Cities, Tribes, States, and Private Businesses 54
International Marine Turtles of Mystery 55
One of these Entitlements is Not Like the Other 56
EPA Power Grab: Final "Waters of the United States" Rule 57
Organizing around the World: Unions for All 59
Going Green, Moroccan Style 60
To Advertise or Not to Advertise? That is the Question. 61
Solar Beer 62

Regulatory Overtime	63
Essential Air Service	64
Federal Protective Service Fleet	65
Cross-Cultural Raisins	66
Indian Coal Country	68
$5,000 Fiddle Film	69
Drug Deals	70
25,000+ Ineligible Families in Public Housing	71
Emergency Spending toward an Emerging Debt Crisis	72
A Different One Percent	73
Government Studies Old Cliché	75
Crime Victims Should Not Be Pawns in Budget Game	76
Fed Study on the Ups and Downs of Senior Dating	77
Out of Sight, Out of Date, Out of Luck	78
EPA's $8.4 Billion "Clean" Power Plan	79
Ambassadors (Slush) Fund	80
Amtrak's Bottomless Pit	81
Taxpayer-Funded Propaganda Machines	82
"I See Dead People."	83
End-of-Year Binge Spending	85
The Hydrology of Hydraulic Fracturing	87
Opportunity Cost: The *Other* Cost of College	88
The Largest and the Highest	89
The 30-Hour Work-Week	91
Solar Burn	92
FEMA Flaws Could Mean Disaster for Disasters	93
Nuclear Waste	94
Advising Advisors	95
Watch out for Snails!	96
The Exception Should Not be the Rule	97
$40 Million to Support "One of the Finest Hotels Anywhere in the World"	98
Taxpayers Get Their Kicks on Route 66	100
Tell Me How Much You Make	102
Identity Theft Tax Fraud	103
Arrest the Office of Juvenile Justice	104
Let Washington, DC, Pick Your Neighborhood	105
Co-Op Collapse	106
Two is Not Better than One	107
Buy More or Fix What You Have?	108
Pricey Empty Rooms	110
NLRB Hates Small Business	112
Corn Squeeze-Ums for Your Car	113
Taxing the World	114
If It Is Worth Doing Once, It Is Worth Doing Eight Times	116
Fool Me Once, Shame On You; Fool Me Twice, Shame On Me	117
Regulations Crush Small, Community Banks	118
Disability is Only for the Disabled	119
Motor Mandates	120
Why Communication Matters	121
Out-of-Control Ozone	123
The Largest Theft of Federal Data in History	124
Touchdown!	126

A $43 MILLION GAS STATION

QUICK STATS

- ✘ **CONFERENCE:** Spending
- ✘ **TEAM:** Department of Defense
- ◯ **FUMBLE:** $42,718,739 gas station in Afghanistan
- ◯ **HOW TO RECOVER THE BALL:** Require DOD to submit reports on all completed facility construction at the one-, three- and five-year marks to certify the facility's use compared to the original construction justification

Photo: Central Asia Development Group

In 2009 DOD moved its Task Force for Business and Stability Operations (TFBSO) from Iraq to Afghanistan.[1] TFBSO's mission was to help build up the economy of war-torn Afghanistan.[2] From 2011-2014 TFBSO spent nearly $43 million in order to construct a CNG automobile filling station in the city of Sheberghan, Afghanistan.[3] The belief was that a CNG station would take advantage of the natural gas reserves within Afghanistan and alleviate the need for importing fuel. Unfortunately TFBSO never vetted the feasibility of such a plan. Had TFBSO vetted the feasibility, it would have determined there was no natural gas distribution capability in the country and that the cost of converting a vehicle to CNG exceeded the annual income in Afghanistan.[4] Would Americans convert their vehicles to run on CNG if it costs more than their annual income? Probably not.

If the outrageous waste of taxpayers' dollars is not enough, DOD was unable to explain the high cost of the project or any other questions regarding its planning. The reason for DOD's inability to provide an explanation is DOD closed TFBSO in March of 2015.[5] During its lifetime TFBSO spent $766 million in taxpayer money, but DOD claims there are no records or expertise on TFBSO's activities.[6]

RECOVERY

DOD should not have wasted this much money on a project that a simple feasibility study would have shown was unnecessary. Congress also should have discovered this wasteful project through simple oversight and brought it to an end. Congress should work with DOD to ensure future investments in other countries advance American interests and actually make a difference. A $43 million natural gas station does neither.

For more information, please visit:
SIGAR: DOD's Compressed Natural Gas Filling Station in Afghanistan: An Ill-Conceived $43 Million Project
Defense News: SIGAR: DoD Spent $43M on 'Ill-Conceived' Afghan Gas Station

SILENT SHAKESPEARE

QUICK STATS

- ✗ **CONFERENCE:** Spending
- ✗ **TEAM:** National Endowment for the Arts
- ○ **FUMBLE:** Tens of thousands of dollars
- ○ **HOW TO RECOVER THE BALL:** Require a thorough disclosure and transparency process for federal grants to ensure funding focuses on items of national interest

In a year when American families had to work 114 days to earn enough money to cover their complete yearly tax bill,[7] NEA awarded a state partner—the Virginia Commission for the Arts—$683,600 for various arts-related projects.[8] The program supported tens of thousands of dollars in funding for <u>silent</u> adaptations of Shakespeare's <u>Hamlet</u> and others at a Washington, DC-area theater.[9] The funding went to support the production costs of the Synetic Theater's taxpayer-funded silent Shakespeare series. Synetic Theater received its highest recent award of $60,700 in 2013 from NEA's partner, Virginia Commission for the Arts.[10] Synetic also received $58,800[11] (2011-2012), $54,900 (2012-2013),[12] and $35,100 (2015-2016).[13]

William Shakespeare was lauded for many things: his meter, his verse, his complicated characters. Generations of families have come together to enjoy productions of Shakespeare's sonnets and plays by film companies, local theaters, and high school drama classes. But was Polonius right in *Hamlet* when he said, "Give every man thy ear, but few thy voice"?

James Bovard published a piece in *The Wall Street Journal* on July 13, 2015, entitled, "A Silenced Shakespeare in Washington: Shakespeare without puns is like French cooking without butter."[14] Performing Shakespeare's plays using private funds or state-funded arts programs might be even "butter."

Photo: Shutterstock

RECOVERY

Congress has allowed NEA to drop the ball in this instance by not providing enough oversight and guidance for federal grants. American families and taxpayers should not work until almost May to earn enough to pay their taxes only to have the government fund grants that are better suited for private or state-based funds. Congress must work to reform the federal grants process to improve transparency and accountability and fulfill its own responsibility of overseeing federal agencies and the federal grants program. National grants should fund national priorities.

For more information, please visit:
Virginia Commission for the Arts – Synetic Theater
Virginia Commission for the Arts – 2015-2016 Grant Awards
Virginia Commission for the Arts – 2013-2014 Grant Awards
Virginia Commission for the Arts – 2012-2013 Grant Awards
Virginia Commission for the Arts – 2011-2012 Grant Awards
The Washington Post: National Endowment for the Arts awards $74 million in grants
The Wall Street Journal: A Silenced Shakespeare in Washington
Tax Foundation: Tax Freedom Day 2015

SUBSIDIZED WIND

QUICK STATS

- ✗ **CONFERENCE:** Spending
- ✗ **TEAM:** Internal Revenue Service
- ○ **FUMBLE:** $6 billion
- ○ **HOW TO RECOVER THE BALL:** End the "temporary" tax incentive after 23 years

Photo: Shutterstock

Even during the hottest part of summer and the coldest part of winter, many families still keep tight control of their home's thermostat. Electric bills can be expensive and difficult to pay.

In 1992 Congress created the Wind Production Tax Credit to kick-start the development of the relatively young wind energy production industry. The credit has changed over the last 23 years, but it currently grants a tax credit of 2.3 cents per kilowatt-hour of energy produced for the first ten years a new wind farm is up and running.[15]

In terms of boosting a relatively young wind industry, the credit has wildly succeeded; wind generation capacity has grown more than 3,000 percent nationwide since it was first put into law.[16] As an example, wind now contributes almost 15 percent of the State of Oklahoma's net power generation.[17] Thirty-eight states have renewable energy portfolio standards, including wind, that are either mandatory or voluntary,[18] and some have financial incentives at the state level as well.

Wind efficiency is up dramatically. This quality energy resource is now fully viable and useful. Every time the credit is extended another year, taxpayers pony up more than $6 billion over ten years for an industry that is already profitable.[19] With trillions in federal debt, this taxpayer money should be used to pay for highways, national defense, or deficit reduction.

RECOVERY

There is no longer a need for a federal subsidy to kick-start wind development; after 23 years it is fully developed. Wind energy has a place in the diverse portfolio of many utilities, but the federal taxpayer should not determine that place. American families, who are already worried about their own bills, should not subsidize the wind as it comes sweepin' down the plain. To protect the taxpayer, I have introduced S. 2158, the PTC Elimination Act, which would permanently eliminate this subsidy from the tax code.

For more information, please visit:
U.S. Energy Information Administration: Oklahoma Profile Overview
U.S. Energy Information Administration: Most States Have Renewable Portfolio Standards
CRS Report: U.S. Renewable Electricity: How Does Wind Generation Impact Competitive Power Markets?
CRS Report: The Renewable Electricity Production Tax Credit: In Brief

A TALE OF WOE, ICE STYLE

QUICK STATS

- ✗ **CONFERENCE:** Spending
- ✗ **TEAM:** Immigration and Customs Enforcement
- ○ **FUMBLE:** $6 million to repair a building that remains unsafe
- ○ **HOW TO RECOVER THE BALL:** ICE should conduct a cost-benefit analysis and a feasibility study before renovating an existing building, where the cost could exceed $1 million

Talk about a tale of woe! In San Pedro (essentially Los Angeles, CA), ICE used a former Service Processing Center to house detainees until it had to close due to safety concerns. Then ICE decided to move employees back into the building while it processed and held illegal immigrants temporarily.

In 2012 USACE found the San Pedro Processing Center to be unsafe and recommended ICE move out completely.[20] In 2014 the IG visited the facility and recommended ICE vacate the building until the safety issues were corrected. ICE finally complied.[21]

Between 2008 and 2014, ICE spent about $4.2 million to repair the building, and it was still unsafe for occupancy when the IG visited in 2014.[22] In 2015 ICE awarded another $1.6 million to retry to make the building safe.[23] Although ICE wanted to repair the entire facility, it failed to develop a long-term plan to address all of the problems with the building. Instead ICE attempted a patchwork of repairs and renovations in a series of small projects. Fast forward to the present day, and ICE still has an unserviceable building at a cost of $6 million.[24]

The tale of woe continues for ICE because the facility may have limited utility moving forward, even if ICE manages to make it safe and serviceable. Since it was designed to hold detainees, there is not enough parking to make it suitable for office space. Worse still, there are no electrical outlets, and the walls are three feet thick.[25]

RECOVERY

Before dropping any additional federal dollars into this building, ICE needs to settle on a long-term plan. Does ICE really need this building, or is it better to just start over? It is frustrating that ICE wasted the $6 million, but demolishing the building and starting over might be more cost-effective in the long run. This tale of woe could have been prevented with a little planning, a cost-benefit analysis, and a basic feasibility study. Everyday Americans know the value of having a plan before starting a big project. Without a plan projects get expensive and inefficient very quickly. It is time the federal government learned the same lesson.

For more information, please visit:
OIG: Follow-up to Management Alert – U.S. Immigration and Customs Enforcement's Facility, San Pedro, California
OIG: Management Alert: Employee Safety at the San Pedro Processing Center

FEDERAL STUDENT LUNCH STANDARDS: THE ANTI-POPEYE

QUICK STATS

- ✗ **CONFERENCE:** Regulation
- ✗ **TEAM:** Department of Agriculture
- ○ **FUMBLE:** Feds prevent schools from adequately feeding students
- ○ **HOW TO RECOVER THE BALL:** Include grain requirements amendment in FY 2016 funding bills and reject centralized meal planning for every school in America

Many American families grew up watching Popeye on television. He would eat his spinach, grow strong, and take on the bad guys. The federal government, evidently wanting all children to grow up with Popeye's healthy eating habits, recently changed federal school lunch requirements with the goal of improving childhood diets and reducing obesity. Unfortunately someone forgot that most kids hate spinach.

Photo: Twitter

To improve childhood diets and reduce obesity, USDA developed nutritional standards under the authority of the Healthy, Hunger-Free Kids Act of 2010. These rules placed limits on the amount of meats and grains permitted in school lunches.

USDA has various rules for school nutritional standards. However, the rules often conflict with each other and are nearly impossible for schools to implement. For example one USDA rule establishes limits for meats in lunches while another sets minimum and maximum calorie requirements for different grades. In schools with multiple grade levels, where the maximum calories allowed for students grades 6-8 (700 calories) are below the minimum calorie requirement for students grades 9-12 (750 calories), schools were forced to develop different meal plans.[26]

The rule also prohibited baked goods with even trace amounts of cornmeal from inclusion in school lunches. As a result, lunchtime staples, such as bagels, may not meet the school nutrition standards. In the end many students chose not to eat the meals they were served because they simply did not like them. Federally mandated lunch standards actually cause many students to not eat enough at lunch. These government meals also do not take into consideration that dietary needs may differ from student to student. A senior offensive lineman on the football team may have different caloric needs than the freshman trumpet player. Families know best what their children should eat for lunch. USDA should not force on schools burdensome meal standards that do not provide enough calories for growing children and are often rejected by students.

RECOVERY

Not surprisingly, GAO found that these regulations were nearly impossible for schools to implement.[27] To improve children's health and nutrition at school, GAO recommended USDA remove the meat and grain limits and allow schools the flexibility to comply with the rules. The U.S. Senate Appropriations Committee addressed GAO's concerns by providing schools with flexibility to meet USDA grain and sodium requirements in its FY 2016 Agriculture Appropriations Bill, which was sent to the full Senate on July 16, 2015.[28] When Congress completes work on the FY 2016 funding bills, this common-sense provision should be included. But since appropriations bills only solve these issues for one year at a time, USDA should step up and provide American schools the flexibility they need to improve the health and nutrition of students, and Congress should reject the notion that Washington, DC, should plan the school lunchroom menu each day. The Founders would be appalled.

For more information, please visit:
GAO: Testimony of Kay E. Brown before the Subcommittee on Early Childhood, Elementary, and Secondary Education, Committee on Education and the Workforce, House of Representatives
S.1800 – Agriculture, Rural Development, Food and Drug Administration, and Related Agencies Appropriations Act, 2016

PAID VACATION, FEDERAL STYLE

QUICK STATS

- ✗ **CONFERENCE:** Spending
- ✗ **TEAM:** Government-wide
- ○ **FUMBLE:** Paying employees on administrative leave for months or even years at a time
- ○ **HOW TO RECOVER THE BALL:** Create a clear process to handle employees on administrative leave; create faster processes for hearings

Leave it to the federal government to find a way to pay people who are not working. The federal government has made it a habit to place workers accused of misconduct on paid administrative leave for months or even years. Yes, years!

GAO released a report in fall 2014 to review the practices of five departments: DOD, VA, USAID, GSA, and DOI. GAO found these departments spent a combined $3.1 billion on workers who were placed on paid administrative leave from 2011 to 2013,[29] $775 million of which went toward the salaries of 57,000 employees who were off work for one month or longer[30]. This is money paid from taxpayers who actually work hard to earn their salaries.

That is a lot of money to waste on not promptly and efficiently handling employee issues. Primarily, workers are placed on leave because they are under investigation for misconduct. Other reasons include whistleblowing and disputes among employees. Even for a complicated case of workplace misconduct, a more efficient and clear process would reduce this extreme waste of time and resources.

Photo: Shutterstock

RECOVERY

Congress should support a clear process for agencies to handle employees who are accused of misconduct or who have been placed on administrative leave for any other reason. If someone receives a paycheck, he or she needs to actually show up for work.

It is not fair to employees to keep them in limbo for months or years, and it is definitely not fair to hard-working American taxpayers to make them foot the bill for agencies that are unable to handle employee issues.

For more information, please visit:
The Fiscal Times: Lawmakers Lash Out at Agencies for Paying $3.1 Billion to Idle Workers
GAO: Federal Paid Administrative Leave: Additional Guidance Needed to Improve OPM Data

DISHWASHER EFFICIENCY STANDARDS

QUICK STATS

- ✗ **CONFERENCE:** Regulation
- ✗ **TEAM:** Department of Energy
- ○ **FUMBLE:** Allow only 3.1 gallons of water to wash a load of dishes
- ○ **HOW TO RECOVER THE BALL:** Work with industry and the public *before* drawing up final regulations

According to the *Merriam-Webster Dictionary*, *efficient* means "capable of producing desired results without wasting materials, time, or energy."[31] Unfortunately, when DOE issued its "higher efficiency standards" for household dishwashers in 2015, they failed to meet the full definition of the word. The new standards, which only allowed 3.1 gallons of water to wash each load of dishes, were issued after already lowering the limit from 6.5 gallons to 5 gallons in 2012.[32,33]

The Association of Home Appliance Manufacturers decided to test the new standards. Accordingly they calibrated their appliances to meet the new standard and ran some tests. The dishwashers that used 3.1 gallons of water ended up with so much residual food on the dishes that they needed to be rewashed to be usable, which completely negates any efficiency achieved. In other words the new standards would save 240 billion gallons of water over a 30-year period and reduce energy consumption by 12 percent, but it would also leave families with dirty dishes that require an additional cycle.[34]

Families already have enough to worry about without adding extra loads of dishes to the mix, simply due to poorly conceived federal regulations. This is another example of a regulation, drawn up in an office building in Washington, DC, that is unworkable for families.

RECOVERY

When the Constitution was written, did the Framers really dream the federal government would one day control how Americans wash their dishes? The constant push for more regulation and efficiency does have a limit. When someone in Washington decides industry must change, the loser is often the consumer who pays higher prices for a less desirable product. The federal government must evaluate products for safety but allow the market and local codes to drive design.

For more information, please visit:
The Hill: Industry rails against Obama's dishwasher rules
Federal Register: Proposed Rules
Fox News: Appliance industry warns federal dishwasher regs would lead to dirty dishes

FEDERAL DIETS

QUICK STATS

- ✗ **CONFERENCE:** Spending
- ✗ **TEAM:** National Institutes of Health
- ○ **FUMBLE:** $2,658,929 weight-loss program for truck drivers
- ○ **RECOVERY:** Congress should develop clearer expectations for areas of research for NIH

The American economy is powered in no small part by the thousands of trucks on the road each day. It is certainly important for individuals behind the wheel of giant 18-wheelers to be healthy. But do taxpayers really need to spend more than $2.6 million on a trucker weight-loss intervention program?

From 2011 to 2015, NIH awarded Oregon Health & Science University a total of $2,658,929 to conduct a cell-phone-based program for a "weight loss competition" and "motivational interviewing."[35] The federal SHIFT program included an initial six-month weight-monitoring program followed by a 30-month follow-up study.[36] The shocking conclusion reached in the 2009 report: individuals who completed motivational interviewing sessions and computer-based training were better able to make healthy living decisions. Those who engaged in the challenging six-month study were then given the chance to participate in a 30-month study.[37]

This extended program was designed to determine whether those who successfully completed the six-month study could maintain a healthier lifestyle without additional motivation or training.[38] Individuals who participated in the program and in the entry phone interview were given a $20 gift card.[39] Participants were then asked to self-report their weight, food intake, and exercise activities over the phone.[40]

RECOVERY

Encouraging people to make healthier living decisions is definitely a good thing that should be done—by doctors, families, and friends, not the federal government and not at a price tag for American taxpayers of $2.6 million over four years.[41] NIH should have thought twice before funding programs when private funding of research studies is a better avenue. Congress, in consultation with NIH and other research institutes, can better assess areas of federal research.

For more information, please visit:
NIH RePORT: Project Information
US National Library of Medicine, NIH: Weight Loss Maintenance Among SHIFT Pilot Study Participants 30-Months Post-Intervention

SAFE HAVENS FOR CRIMINALS

QUICK STATS

- ✗ **CONFERENCE:** Regulation (lost trust)
- ✗ **TEAM:** Multiple localities, states, and federal immigration enforcement
- ○ **FUMBLE:** Failing to enforce immigration detainer orders
- ○ **HOW TO RECOVER THE BALL:** Congress should pass legislation to prohibit sanctuary cities

Generally sanctuary cities are localities throughout the U.S. with policies that prohibit or restrict local police or law enforcement cooperation with federal immigration efforts. There are two problems. First, there is no universal definition of the term *sanctuary city*, and it can be used to define many different types of activities. Second, these non-cooperation policies allow criminals to be released back onto the streets, potentially endangering American lives.

On July 1, 2015, Kathryn Steinle was fatally shot in San Francisco by an illegal immigrant who was previously convicted of seven felonies and was previously deported on five occasions. What makes her tragic story worse is that the illegal immigrant should have already been deported for a sixth time. In fact immigration officials had him in custody before transferring him to the San Francisco Sheriff's Department on charges of drug possession. Immigration officials then issued a detainer, which requests notification before a prisoner is released, so they could deport him. But San Francisco, a sanctuary city by its own definition, decided not to notify immigration officials and released the prisoner after choosing not to charge him for drug possession.

Releasing criminals who could otherwise be deported is a common occurrence. In 2014 approximately 12,000 detainers[42] were ignored by cities around the nation. Sanctuary city policies that ignore crimes committed by illegal immigrants are unacceptable, and the policies directly lead to consequences like the murder of Kathryn Steinle. Most illegal immigrants are not murderers or criminals, but those who are criminals should not be released into American communities to commit additional crimes.

RECOVERY

Congress should pass legislation to prohibit sanctuary cities and reaffirm that immigration policies are determined at the national level, not by cities and counties. Congress should also set firm consequences for illegal re-entry into the country, particularly for those with criminal convictions. It should not be controversial to remove illegal felons from the United States.

For more information, please visit:
CRS Report: Sanctuary Jurisdictions and Criminal Aliens: In Brief
Los Angeles Times: Sanctuary Cities: How Kathryn Steinle's death intensified the immigration debate

GOT GNATCATCHERS?

QUICK STATS

- **CONFERENCE:** Spending
- **TEAM:** Department of Defense
- **FUMBLE:** $283,500 gnatcatcher survey
- **HOW TO RECOVER THE BALL:** Congress should establish a policy that all grants issued by the Department of Defense must support national security

FWS listed the coastal CAGN, a tiny blue-gray bird, as a "threatened" species in 1993. Earlier this year, DOD issued a grant worth $283,500 to survey "at least ten California gnatcatcher (CAGN) pairs in order to determine use throughout each vegetation alliance." Thankfully DOD provides an explanation for this, which includes monitoring of CAGN nests, the ability of baby CAGNs to learn to fly, and the temperature and availability of food around the nest. The surveyor would also document any instances of cowbirds, another small bird, laying eggs in CAGN nests. (Note: Evidently the Cowbirds tend to do this for some reason.) [43]

In what universe should DOD spend $283,500 to study the day-to-day life of a tiny bird? How is American national security strengthened by this study? DOD should be in the business of defense, not nature conservancy. First, there is an entire federal agency that does things like this: FWS. Second, any project like this, regardless of the agency in charge, should always have to publically demonstrate the purpose and rationale for any grant, and publicly release the findings afterwards.

Photo: Shutterstock

RECOVERY

Congress should work with DOD to ensure there are no federal restrictions to the Department remaining completely focused on keeping the homeland safe. DOD should not feel obligated to fulfill the mission of other federal agencies. It has a tough enough job already.

For more information, please visit:
Grants.gov: Coastal California Gnatcatcher Habitat Use Study and Population Surveys at Marine Corps Air Station Miramar, California
U.S. Fish & Wildlife Service: Coastal California Gnatcatcher

CMS FILES SECRETIVE SETTLEMENT

QUICK STATS

- **CONFERENCE:** Regulation
- **TEAM:** Centers for Medicare and Medicaid Services
- **FUMBLE:** $1.3 Billion
- **HOW TO RECOVER THE BALL:** Congress should work with CMS to solve the backlog issues that result in a $1.3 billion settlement

Here is a story about federal inefficiency that also cost American families a lot of money and could ultimately result in higher costs and fewer providers. When Medicare and Medicaid patients go to a doctor or a hospital, a claim is filed and, if considered eligible for reimbursement, the bill is paid directly to that doctor or hospital. If the claim is denied for any reason, the hospital has the right to appeal. Here is where the problem starts: CMS has such a dysfunctional, disorganized, and backlogged system that it cannot properly process the appeals. So instead of taking the time to actually fix its system, CMS just agreed to partially pay all the hospitals who appeal an already denied claim.

In June 2015 CMS settled for $1.3 billion with 1,900 hospitals and paid 300,000 claims previously deemed "medically unnecessary," which were already reviewed and denied twice.[44] Most of these claims were related to short inpatient stays, which have long been a source of abuse and improper claims. But worst of all, CMS paid these settlements from the Medicare Trust Fund without telling anyone or asking permission.[45] Those who rely on Medicaid and Medicare deserve CMS to be a good steward in administering the programs, and taxpayers deserve to know their hard-earned dollars are spent appropriately. A major part of the problem is this: the system of auditing the providers has so many problems and mistakes that good providers are treated like criminals instead of public servants. When a provider is forced to prove innocence, enormous numbers of appeals and a huge backlog are created.

RECOVERY

Congress should immediately investigate how CMS got to this point, why major changes were not made, and how a more than $1 billion settlement could be made without congressional approval. This cannot happen again. American families cannot afford it, and good healthcare providers should not have to endure it.

For more information, please visit:
CMS: Inpatient Hospital Reviews
The Washington Free Beacon: CMS' Secretive Settlement
Citizens Against Government Waste: CAGW Slams CMS for Secretive Settlement, Payments of $1.3 Billion for Improper Hospital Claims

A $4 MILLION REBEL

QUICK STATS

- ✘ **CONFERENCE:** Spending
- ✘ **TEAM:** Department of Defense
- ◯ **FUMBLE:** $250 million to train 60 Syrian rebels
- ◯ **HOW TO RECOVER THE BALL:** Require DOD to continually evaluate programs and move more quickly to eliminate programs that do not meet expectations

Last year, Congress gave $500 million in federal tax money to train and provide equipment for at least 5,400 Syrian rebels fighting against ISIL. Over the next year, DOD spent about half of that amount and managed to train an overwhelming force of 60 fighters. In other words DOD spent about $4 million per rebel.[46]

This resounding lack of success is likely why on October 9, 2015, the Obama Administration announced a "pause" in the program to re-evaluate how the U.S. would support those fighting against ISIL.[47] In a press release, DOD announced it would begin to provide equipment and weapons to select rebel leaders instead of training them.

RECOVERY

It is good DOD finally recognized that this training and equipping program did not work. However, it should not have taken a year and $250 million to figure that out. DOD should have evaluated this program at every stage rather than wait a year to decide its fate. The federal government absolutely needs to support those who fight on the ground against this terrorist group. But Americans deserved to get more for their tax money. A clear Syria strategy is long overdue from this White House. Americans can see the obvious threat, and most Americans understand that sending 60 rebels into Syria at a cost of $4 million each is not a winning strategy.

For more information, please visit:
United States Senate Committee on Armed Services: Counter-ISIL Strategy
US Department of Defense: Statement on Syria
Politico: Price Tag for Syrian Rebels: $4 million each
CNN: U.S. suspending program to train and equip Syrian rebels

ACADEMY AWARDS MUSEUM SUBSIDY

QUICK STATS

- ✗ **CONFERENCE:** Spending
- ✗ **TEAM:** National Endowment for the Arts
- ○ **FUMBLE:** $25,000 for a grant to fund the Oscars museum
- ○ **HOW TO RECOVER THE BALL:** Increased oversight of the award-making process

And the Oscar for Hollywood's best supporting government agency goes to...the NEA!

NEA announced in April that it would award a $25,000 grant to the Academy of Motion Picture and Science's planned museum. According to NEA, the grant will support the planning of the historical exhibition and specifically will "solidify content and interpretive strategies to build on a series of design charrettes held with filmmakers, artists, scholars, and experts in a range of disciplines that helped to define the exhibition's interpretive approaches."[48] The $388 million museum, which is expected to open in 2017, aspires to "celebrate the rich history of Hollywood and filmmaking worldwide and will take a look behind the screen at the artistry and technological creativity that have made those unforgettable cinematic moments possible."[49]

While film buffs are likely elated by the planned museum, most Americans will question the need for their tax dollars to help roll out the red carpet for the well-heeled organization. For instance the fundraising campaign for the museum was able to generate $250 million in "record time."[50] In the summer of 2014, the project managers expanded the fundraising goal by $50 million to create "really expansive and immersive exhibitions and programs within the museum, and then arriving at some contingencies just to buffer the budget and give us a little bit of flexibility."[51] Not only does the Academy have an impressive capacity to fundraise from donors, it has a tremendous amount of internal revenue-generating capability. In 2013 the Academy of Motion Picture Arts and Sciences generated $101.5 million in revenues, primarily through the Oscars, and held a net asset balance of $231.5 million.[52] Given its substantial financial prowess, the fact that the Academy even applied for a federal grant is disconcerting. The fact that it was awarded is unconscionable.

Photo: Shutterstock/MidoSemsem

RECOVERY

Supporting the arts is a noble endeavor. In this case American moviegoers already contribute significant support to the box office every year to enjoy their favorite Hollywood stars and storylines. They should not be expected to contribute their tax dollars as well.

For more information, please visit:
National Endowment for the Arts: FY2015 Spring Grant Announcement
Oscars: About
Los Angeles Times: Film academy's museum gets $25,000 grant from the NEA
Hollywood Reporter: Academy Museum Fundraising Chief to Step Down
Guidestar: Return of Organization Exempt from Income Tax

RUSSIAN CIGARETTES

QUICK STATS

- ✘ **CONFERENCE:** Spending
- ✘ **TEAM:** National Institutes of Health
- ◯ **FUMBLE:** $48,500 to study the history of tobacco use in Russia
- ◯ **HOW TO RECOVER THE BALL:** Utilize resources to provide greater public health outcomes

NIH's stated mission is "to seek fundamental knowledge about the nature and behavior of living systems and the application of that knowledge to enhance health, lengthen life, and reduce illness and disability."[53] Perhaps running counter to the mission, in April 2015 NIH announced a $48,500 grant to produce a book entitled, *Cigarettes and Soviets: The Culture of Tobacco Use in Modern Russia*.[54] While the title harkens images of a James Bond movie, the grant will go to pay a historian to write "the first solo-authored monograph in Russian or English to explore the history of tobacco use and government-initiated cessation programs in Russia in the context of the country's complex social, cultural, and political changes of the past 130 years."[55]

In order to compile the book, the author will "reconstruct the culture of tobacco using newspapers, journals, industry publications, etiquette manuals, propaganda posters, popular literature, films, cartoons, and advertising images." The supposed hook into NIH and public health relevance is that "understanding Russia's distinctive history may suggest different strategies for U.S. policy initiatives" and that it can "provide insights into the successes and failures of government-led tobacco control efforts." While subjective, it is likely that most taxpayers would find the merits of the history of Russian smoking habits outside the scope of NIH's mission and American national interests.[56]

RECOVERY

Recently NIH made major medical advances in Ebola research, gene therapy to treat hemophilia, blood tests for early detection of Alzheimer's. Four men even regained muscle control from paralysis after spinal stimulation therapy.[57] These advances truly make a difference and help families across the nation. Instead of funding the publication of niche history books, Congress should push NIH to continue to concentrate its resources on more transformative research to provide public health breakthroughs for the American people. Leave the study of Russian cigarettes to the Russians.

For more information, please visit:
NIH: Mission and Goals
Grantome: Cigarettes and Soviets: The Culture of Tobacco Use in Modern Russia
NIH Office of History: Selected Research Advances of NIH

TOY GUNS: REGULATORY HOTSPOT

QUICK STATS

- ✘ **CONFERENCE:** Regulation
- ✘ **TEAM:** National Institute of Standards and Technology and Customs and Border Protection
- ○ **FUMBLE:** Duplicative toy gun regulations
- ○ **HOW TO RECOVER THE BALL:** Congress should transfer the oversight to one agency for enforcement; OMB should eliminate regulatory duplication

Photo: Shutterstock

When asked to think of an industry that faces particularly duplicative and complex federal regulations, the financial or energy sectors come to mind first for most Americans. However, the federal government's arm extends into every industry, including toy gun manufacturers and importers. It is important to ensure the safety of every child, but perhaps it can be done in a more efficient manner without sacrificing safety. GAO's 2015 annual report to Congress on federal duplication and overlap describes multiple examples of duplicative regulations, but the toy gun industry example stands out in particular.

In order to distinguish toy guns from real firearms, NIST within DOC holds primary regulatory jurisdiction over toy guns and imitation firearms.[58] This is a serious and important safety responsibility to protect the lives of millions of children. However, the 2015 GAO report found an interesting loophole in the regulatory structure of the toy gun industry, confirmed by the regulating agency itself: "NIST staff also noted that because there are few, if any, domestic manufacturers of toy and imitation firearms and because most are imported, NIST regulations on the markings for toy and imitation firearms are enforced almost entirely by Customs and Border Protection (CBP)." GAO also noted the possibility for inefficiency, stating that "because the regulation of toy and imitation firearms falls outside the scope of NIST's primary mission and functions and because NIST has no physical presence at ports of entry, NIST staff stated the regulation and oversight of toy and imitation firearm markings may better be administered by another federal agency."[59]

The difference between a toy gun and a real gun can result in fatal consequences. When it comes to children's safety, the federal government must get this right.

RECOVERY

The regulating authority of the toy gun industry should be transferred to the entity that actually has enforcement capability: CBP. Removing duplicative responsibilities will ensure regulations are implemented appropriately and keep toy costs low for parents.

For more information, please visit:
GAO: 2015 Annual Report: Additional Opportunities to Reduce Fragmentation, Overlap, and Duplication and Achieve Other Financial Benefits
GPO: Electronic Code of Federal Regulations

THE TRUTH IS NOT CHEAP

QUICK STATS

- ✘ **CONFERENCE:** Spending
- ✘ **TEAM:** Department of State
- ✪ **FUMBLE:** $545,000 for truth-telling consultants
- ✪ **RECOVERY:** Departments should be more selective in the types of training grants they offer; activities that can be handled internally should be handled internally

The cost of telling the truth? Apparently, it is $545,000 at State.[60] In March 2014 State's School of Leadership and Management sought a contractor to provide training courses to "senior level officials on effective congressional testimony and briefing skills."[61] The name of the course? "Communicating with Congress: Briefing and Testifying."[62] Additionally the contractor would assist with the design of congressional testimony prep classes for individuals who are nominated to be ambassadors and one-on-one classes for individuals set to testify before Congress.

Photo: Shutterstock

So basically American taxpayers paid more than $500,000 to have a contractor teach people how to sit before a congressional committee and answer questions.

It is understandable that State wants to prepare its witnesses, perhaps to avoid embarrassing situations such as the nominee-to-be Ambassador to China saying, "I'm no real expert on China" or its nominee for the U.S. representative in Norway who testified about the non-existent president of that country.[63] But does the federal government really need to hire an outside contractor to train federal officials and nominees on how to testify before Congress and tell the truth? Surely not.

RECOVERY

Congress should use its oversight responsibilities to guide federal agencies (not contractors) to handle training or other internal matters that could be undertaken by staff already on the federal payroll. Another idea is to tell all State Department staff to just honor any mom's advice, "When in doubt, tell the truth."

For more information, please visit:
The Washington Times: State Department hires testimony coach to prepare for congressional grillings
Federal Business Opportunities: Congressional Training

TAXPAYER-FUNDED MEDIA ETHICS IN INDIA

QUICK STATS

- ✗ **CONFERENCE:** Spending
- ✗ **TEAM:** Department of State
- ○ **FUMBLE:** $25,000 for media ethics training in India
- ○ **HOW TO RECOVER THE BALL:** Suspend the grant program

State's Diplomatic Mission to India announced in July 2015 that it sought proposals for a media ethics course for journalists in India under the culturally relevant "Blurred Lines" moniker.[64] Since Indian journalists are "part of a global community of media professionals," as the ad put it, the course would supply "a baseline understanding of the international industry standards media should strive to meet."[65] In other words State believes American taxpayers should sponsor a program to teach Indian journalists how to be journalists.

A free and open press is such an undeniable right in the U.S. that it is one of the first protections in the Constitution. Americans should welcome the press corps of other countries to adopt the best habits of the American press corps. But that does not mean American families should pay for it.

RECOVERY

Americans are among the most philanthropic people in the world. There are plenty of opportunities for individual journalists, universities, and corporations to spread their organizational knowledge to other countries. Congress should work with State to ensure grant money does not duplicate work the private sector could do instead.

For more information, please visit:
Grants.gov: Blurred Lines: A Media Ethics Course for Indian Journalists
The Weekly Standard: State Dept. to Offer Course on Ethics for Journalists: 'Blurred Lines'

CAUTION: READ BEFORE EATING!

QUICK STATS

- **CONFERENCE:** Regulation
- **TEAM:** Food and Drug Administration
- **FUMBLE:** $1 billion cost in the first year alone for new menu and product-labeling nutrition guides
- **HOW TO RECOVER THE BALL:** Allow restaurants and grocery stores to continue labeling food as they do today or list details on their website

Photo: Shutterstock

You are what you eat, and the federal government wants to make sure you know it. Starting December 1, 2015, an FDA rule will require all restaurants, gas stations, entertainment venues, and grocery stores with 20 or more locations to list the total caloric value of the prepared food and drinks they sell.[66] For example Domino's Pizza, which already posts its nutrition information online, will be required to develop new labels with caloric values for every pizza sold. Domino's and Pizza Hut will be forced to label more than five million potential custom pizza options with specific caloric intake information, costing individual stores thousands of dollars.

Grocery stores will also be required to list the caloric values of prepared foods they serve that are intended to be eaten immediately. According to the Food Marketing Institute, this new rule could cost the grocery industry a colossal $1 billion in compliance in the first year alone.[67] Since these institutions will simply pass along the increased costs to consumers, the immediate result of the new menu labels will be higher food prices for consumers. Families will pay more for food purchased at grocery stores and for pizza they order for dinner.

RECOVERY

Trust Americans to pick the food they like and want. Drop the entire labeling requirement. If all of the menu labeling cannot be eliminated, at least consider Rep. Cathy McMorris Rodgers's (WA) Common Sense Nutrition Disclosure Act of 2015, which will provide flexibilities to restaurants to include either the number of calories contained in a whole menu item or the number of servings and calories per serving. Additionally the Act would allow nutritional information to be provided on an Internet menu for food establishments where the majority of orders are delivery or takeout.[68]

For more information, please visit:
Federal Register: Food Labeling; Nutrition Labeling of Standard Menu Items in Restaurants and Similar Retail Food Establishments
The Hill: FDA rolls out ObamaCare menu regs
H.R. 2017 – Common Sense Nutrition Disclosure Act of 2015

LLAMAGATE

QUICK STATS

- ✗ **CONFERENCE:** Regulation
- ✗ **TEAM:** Department of Agriculture
- ○ **FUMBLE:** Inflexible regulations threaten therapy llamas and common sense
- ○ **HOW TO RECOVER THE BALL:** The federal government should stop engaging in permitting processes that are the responsibilities of state and local officials

Photo: Bryan Berky

In February 2015 two llamas quickly became an Internet sensation when they escaped from their farm in Phoenix, AZ. Soon after the llamas escaped, people around the country tracked their movements via social media until they were safely returned home.

Nine years before they had their 15 minutes of fame on cable news networks, the owners, Bub Bullis and Karen Freund, started raising llamas to use as therapy animals for the elderly and for educational purposes. Shortly after the February incident, USDA officials contacted the owners to inform them they needed a license to "showcase" their llamas, even if people only took a few pictures with the llamas.[69]

The owners repeatedly called USDA to try to follow up on the matter but were informed the agency only responds to written inquiries. Eventually the owners stopped showcasing their llamas to avoid the risk of facing fines. As a result, Ms. Freund said, "They [USDA] just totally destroyed everything I had planned for my retirement."[70] Citizens who reach out to their government for help should receive that help and not a cold shoulder.

RECOVERY

Why does a llama need permission from someone in Washington, DC, to smile for a camera? State and local permits should suffice. Americans want safe schools for children and clean retirement facilities for the elderly. What Americans do not want is an inflexible and distant permitting process. When a citizen calls a federal agency for assistance, the citizen should never be told the federal agency cannot help him or her unless the problem is submitted in writing. Americans do not work for the federal government; the federal government works for Americans. Obtaining a livestock permit should not be more complicated than capturing a llama on the loose, and it should not be the business of the federal government.

For more information, please visit:
The Guardian: USDA herding internet's celebrity llamas out of the spotlight, owners say
USDA: Regulated Businesses (Licensing and Registration)

STAND-BY FOR DELIVERY (MAYBE)

QUICK STATS

- ✗ **CONFERENCE:** Spending
- ✗ **TEAM:** Department of Defense
- ○ **FUMBLE:** $48 million in military supplies for Yemen that never made it out of a Virginia warehouse
- ○ **RECOVERY:** Ensure supplies can be delivered and utilized as intended before purchase

Expired medical supplies, corroded batteries, and low-grade explosives for airplane ejection seats are only a small portion of the $48 million worth of American taxpayer-financed supplies intended for Yemen that never reached their intended destination.[71] Instead these items sit in a warehouse in Virginia.

Since 2007 DOD in conjunction with State has strived "to build Yemen's capacity to counter terrorist threats, expand governance throughout its territory, and secure its infrastructure and population."[72] Home to AQAP, Yemen is a frequent target of U.S. interests at home and abroad.[73] Americans' safety and security depends on the ability to neutralize threats in Yemen before they take shape. To that end the U.S. allocated $108 million in Foreign Military Financing funding to Yemen, $48 million of which was actually spent.[74] According to GAO, of the equipment purchased with the $48 million from American taxpayers, various articles remain stored, unused, and unshipped due to a dispute between the Government of Yemen and its freight shipper.[75] Between 2007 and 2012, a variety of mishaps, including contract disputes and late payments, resulted in commercial shippers not moving the items from Virginia to Yemen.[76] In 2012 Yemen ultimately started to pay the U.S. military to directly ship items still deemed useable but left many others behind.[77]

RECOVERY

Any foreign aid should accomplish a goal of increased American security. Americans do not want our money wasted. Going forward, Congress should work with DOD to ensure that when supplies are purchased to aid another country, there is a vetted plan to deliver them in a timely manner and that delivery actually occurs. This plan should include what to do with the supplies, if they become undeliverable. American families, many of whom struggle to afford their own basic needs, should not have to foot the bill for unused supplies intended for other countries.

For more information, please visit:
GAO: Security Assistance: Taxpayer Funds Spent on Equipment that was Never Shipped to Yemen
The Washington Post: More than $600,000 dollars in Yemeni military aid found in a Virginia warehouse

MORE MONEY, FEWER RESULTS

QUICK STATS

✘ **CONFERENCE:** Spending
✘ **TEAM:** Department of Health and Human Services
○ **FUMBLE:** $4 billion
○ **RECOVERY:** No funds for failed state exchanges; repeal Obamacare

Under Obamacare states were given the option to set up their own health insurance exchanges to buy and sell insurance or to allow the federal government to operate an exchange within the state. Fourteen states and the District of Columbia established their own exchanges. The Obama Administration, eager to support their efforts, shelled out $4 billion[78] from taxpayers for planning, establishment, and innovator exchange grants—more than the federal government spent on the nationwide federally facilitated marketplace.

Most taxpayers would reasonably expect that a higher investment would yield a higher return, but that was not the case. When the 14 states that established exchanges opened for business, seven were dysfunctional, disabled, or severely underperforming.[79] For example Oregon's exchange failed to enroll a single person through its online platform, despite spending $304 million[80] in taxpayer dollars. Oregon eventually gave up and turned its exchange over to the federal government. Maryland's exchange failed almost as soon as it launched. Massachusetts, which already had a functioning state website for health insurance, received $184 million[81] in federal funds for a boondoggle that flopped so spectacularly during its first open enrollment that its executive director "wept at a board meeting, where it was disclosed that 50,000 applications for health insurance are sitting in a pile, and have yet to be entered into a computer system."[82] Obamacare, "despite all the massive brainpower behind it, had some 'glitches,' in the same sense that the universe has some 'atoms.'"[83]

So where did all of the money go? GAO reports, "[T]he specific amount spent on marketplace-related projects was uncertain, as only a selected number of states reported to GAO that they tracked or estimated this information."[84]

RECOVERY

Unimpressed by this display of spending malfeasance and mismanagement, Congress declined to offer further funds for state exchanges. The entire system continues to drive up healthcare costs and healthcare complexities. It is time to stop wasting Americans' money on a failed policy.

For more information, please visit:
Reason: Obamacare's Failed State Exchanges
Senate Republican Policy Committee: Obamacare's Embarrassing and Costly State Exchange Flops
CRS: Federal Funding for Health Insurance Exchanges
GAO: State Health Insurance Marketplaces: CMS Should Improve Oversight of State Information Technology Projects

AND WHILE WE ARE AT IT

QUICK STATS

- ✘ **CONFERENCE:** Spending
- ✘ **TEAM:** Centers for Medicare and Medicaid Services
- ⭕ **FUMBLE:** $30,000 per year, per fake enrollee
- ⭕ **HOW TO RECOVER THE BALL:** Cooperation with congressional investigators, corrective guidance and regulations, and/or legislation

Among the many promises made to the American people during the Obamacare debate, the Administration was very clear that only qualified low-income Americans would receive subsidies. It turns out that promise was not kept either.

As part of a "secret shopper" investigation commissioned by Congress to test Obamacare's eligibility enrollment controls, GAO created 18 fictitious identities to apply for premium subsidies under Obamacare. All but one of the fake applicants were able to obtain premium tax credits through telephone and online applications, despite not actually being real people. The cost for a fake applicant's subsidy per year is $30,000. And when it came time to re-enroll at the end of 2014, 11 of the false applicants were able to extend their coverage. In some cases those applicants were able to obtain an even more generous tax credit using just the information they provided during the initial application.[85]

RECOVERY

Absent a repeal of Obamacare, CMS, which oversees the implementation of Obamacare, should cooperate with congressional investigators and GAO to determine how fake applicants can get tax credits.

For more information, please visit:
GAO: Preliminary Results of Undercover Testing of Enrollment Controls for Health Care Coverage and Consumer Subsidies Provided Under the Act
The Wall Street Journal: ObamaCare Undercover

GETTING DRESSED, *JETSONS* STYLE

QUICK STATS

- ✗ **CONFERENCE:** Spending
- ✗ **TEAM:** National Science Foundation
- ◯ **FUMBLE:** $1.2 million for a robotic dresser
- ◯ **HOW TO RECOVER THE BALL:** Require a thorough disclosure and transparency process for federal grants to ensure funding focuses on items of national interest

Parents around the nation know the daily struggle of picking out clothes and ensuring their young children get dressed each day before school. It seems NSF believes the challenge does not get easier with age. NSF has spent nearly $1.2 million to teach robots how to choose outfit combinations for and dress the elderly. NSF anticipates spending at least four years to work through the kinks.[86]

RECOVERY

American families love television shows like *The Jetsons* because they provide good, wholesome entertainment for all ages. However, American taxpayers do not want to see their hard-earned dollars funding projects that try to bring *The Jetsons* to life. The robotic dresser is only the newest project in a long line of NSF efforts to create robotic helpers, all funded by taxpayers. Congress needs to clearly define research priorities for the NSF to help protect taxpayer dollars. Incredible technological advancements can come from simple research, but not every idea needs taxpayer money as the national debt moves toward $19 trillion.

For more information, please visit:
NSF: Robotic Assistance with Dressing using Simulation-Based Optimization
The Washington Free Beacon: Feds Spend $1.2 Million for Robots to Dress Old People

NO ROCKS FOR WARS

QUICK STATS

- ✗ **CONFERENCE:** Regulation
- ✗ **TEAM:** Securities and Exchange Commission
- ○ **FUMBLE:** $3 to 4 billion cost in the first year for mineral tracking
- ○ **HOW TO RECOVER THE BALL:** Congress should re-address conflict minerals

The Dodd-Frank Act, a massive 2,300-page financial regulation law enacted in 2010, does more than complicate business for community banks. As directed under Section 1502 of this law, SEC created a regulation on the use of conflict minerals originating in the DRC.[87] Conflict minerals are any minerals (for example, gold or tin) that can be sold to finance a country's internal conflict.

Conflict minerals have been sold for decades to finance the generations-long conflict within the DRC. This rule's intended goals are to prevent DRC conflict minerals from being used by American companies and to reduce conflict in this war-torn region. SEC estimated the rule will affect 6,000 companies and cost the companies a combined $3 billion to $4 billion in the first year with at least $200 million in costs each year thereafter. Designed to remove conflict minerals from U.S. supply chains, the rule acknowledges it will not "generate measurable, direct economic benefits," and SEC estimates that generating these reports will require 5.6 million paperwork-reporting hours per year.

A recent *Washington Post* article describes how this well-intentioned rule may have actually exacerbated the situation. In an effort to comply with the regulation, the Congolese government shut down portions of the mining industry and launched a program to certify that the country's minerals were "conflict-free." However, the certification program was plagued with corruption, and many foreign companies stopped purchasing Congolese minerals, forcing former miners to find new jobs, including joining armed rebel groups, which only deepened unemployment and the conflict.[88]

Under the rule DOC is required to publish a list of conflict mineral smelters for the affected companies to use when completing this rule's required paperwork. But in 2014 GAO revealed this simple metric was still not issued in time to provide guidance to the companies.[89] While Americans want to see this violent conflict end, they do not want their government creating costly regulations that do little to solve the conflict or—even worse—exacerbate it.

American companies now file complicated conflict mineral forms and can face stiff fines if they do not file the conflict form saying they have no conflict minerals. Yes, a company faces huge fines if it does not report that it has nothing to report.

RECOVERY

We can all agree conflict minerals fuel the conflict in unstable portions of eastern DRC, and American companies should not purchase conflict minerals. However, the rule fails to achieve any tangible results and creates more chaos and confusion, while costing American businesses billions of dollars. To fix this mistake, Congress should re-examine more effective ways to prevent the purchase of conflict minerals by American companies.

For more information, please visit:
GAO: Conflict Minerals: Stakeholder Options for Responsible Sourcing Are Expanding, but More Information on Smelters Is Needed
DOC: Conflict Mineral Report
SEC: Conflict Minerals Final Rule
SEC: Form SD Specialized Disclosure Report
The Washington Post: In Congo, trapped in violence and forgotten

BIG BILLBOARDS, BIGGER REGULATIONS

QUICK STATS

- ✘ **CONFERENCE:** Regulation
- ✘ **TEAM:** Department of Transportation
- ○ **FUMBLE:** Broad highway regulations threaten Times Square billboards
- ○ **HOW TO RECOVER THE BALL:** Regulators need to calculate the unintended consequences of their regulations prior to implementation

Times Square in New York City is one of America's most iconic locations, but even it is not protected from an uncertain regulatory environment. Broadway and 7th Avenue, which combine to form Times Square, are classified as major arterial roads under the 2012 Moving Ahead for Progress in the 21st Century Act (MAP-21) by the National Highway System. They are also packed with large, iconic billboards. The 1965 Highway Beautification Act limits signage along the National Highway System to 1,200 square feet or less. This 1965 law, originally intended to prevent huge billboards from obstructing views along interstates in primarily rural areas, presents an unfortunate side effect for many of the Times Square billboards that are significantly larger than the 1,200 square-foot limit and subjected to federal scrutiny.[90]

FHWA stated, "The penalty for not providing effective control of outdoor advertising remains at 10 percent of the funds that would otherwise be apportioned to the State."[91] The future of these iconic billboards, which serve as a backdrop for countless tourists, remained uncertain for several months this year until FHWA stated the billboards would not be removed, funding would not be reduced, and an agreement *would* be negotiated. However, uncertainty still exists for New York City and others because no final resolution has been announced by the federal government.

Photo: Sean Pavone/Shutterstock

RECOVERY

It is time for DC to stop telling every city and state how large or small their road signs can be. Millions of American families visit New York City each year to enjoy Times Square and its glowing billboards. The existence of lucrative American landmarks like these billboards (a *Wall Street Journal* article noted that one billboard alone brought in $23 million annually) should not be threatened by federal regulators, especially when the original law did not intend to impact them.[92] Regulators should provide cities and businesses with common-sense flexibility. Congress should also work with FHWA to bring long-term certainty to Times Square and the nation by eliminating this regulation.

For more information, please visit:
Federal Highway Administration: National Highway System Questions and Answers
The Washington Post: How the federal government could use conditional spending to force the removal of Times Square billboards (UPDATED)
The Wall Street Journal: Ads, Not Tenants, Make Times $quare

PONY PALS: WILD HORSES OF THE WILD WEST

QUICK STATS

- ✗ **CONFERENCE:** Spending
- ✗ **TEAM:** Bureau of Land Management
- ○ **FUMBLE:** $67.9 million for wild horse management
- ○ **HOW TO RECOVER THE BALL:** Transfer the management and care of the wild horse and burro populations to private entities

Photo: Facebook – BLM Wild Hourse & Burro Program

The image of majestic wild horses—manes flowing against the backdrop of a blazing sunset—may be a romantic reminder of the Old American West. But the truth is that these creatures are feral descendants of animals that escaped from or were turned loose over the centuries by Spanish explorers, settlers, miners, Native American Tribes, and the U.S. cavalry. Because wild horses and burros (WHBs) have virtually no natural enemies, they have adapted and thrived. For decades the population of these majestic creatures was kept in check by rounding them up to sell for slaughter—until 1950 when Velma Bronn Johnston, a.k.a. "Wild Horse Annie," began a crusade to end what she saw as the inhumane removal of WHBs. The persistence of Mrs. Johnston and other horse lovers led to the Hunting Wild Horses and Burros on Public Lands Act of 1959 and the Wild Free-Roaming Horses and Burros Act of 1971,[93] which gave these wild animals protected status and mandated BLM and the Forest Service to manage, protect, and control WHBs on public lands.[94]

To comply with the law, BLM must conduct an annual census of WHBs roaming the 179 Herd Management Areas in the West—a vast area of 26.9 million acres. BLM must also determine the number of animals the managed areas can reasonably sustain. In March 2015 for example, an estimated 58,150 WHBs roamed ranges able to tolerate just 26,715. Every year the population of animals exceeds what the land can handle, and some of the surplus WHBs are rounded up and removed to off-range pastures and corrals, such as the holding facility in Pauls Valley, OK. Once in these facilities, the animals are available for sale or adoption, but the number of willing adopters of wild horses falls short of the number of horses in excess. Animals that are passed up for adoption three times are transferred to long-term, off-range contract facilities, 20 of which are in Oklahoma.

However, this is only a stopgap measure, as WHBs are prolific reproducers whose numbers double about every four years in captivity. BLM has tried various forms of birth control in an attempt to thin the herds, but no effective, easily-administered remedy has yet been developed. As a result, the off-range population alone has continued to climb to an October

2015 count of 47,204 animals to care for and feed for the rest of their lives.[95]

But should the federal government be in the business of managing WHBs anyway? There are numerous privately funded organizations already dedicated to looking out for their interests. Surely these groups could oversee and protect WHBs more efficiently than BLM, which recently released a report showing that, contrary to BLM policy, a private buyer managed to purchase 1,794 wild horses that were ultimately sold to other buyers. The animals were in turn sold to Mexican slaughterhouses.[96] The current federal program clearly requires ever-increasing diligence and man hours to find, count, round up, protect, and otherwise manage the animals.

Plus, it is just plain expensive. In FY 2014 alone, costs for the program totaled $67.9 million, 63 percent of which went to off-range holding expenses at a cost of almost $4 per day, per animal.[97]

RECOVERY

Of course Americans believe in protecting all of God's creatures, but people come first. The U.S. should stop paying to care for and feed wild animals and allow humane, private-sector solutions to manage the WHB population.

Or alternatively give every American child a free pony on his or her 8th birthday (feed and saddle not included).

For more information visit:
BLM: Wild Horses and Burro Quick Facts
GAO: Bureau of Land Management: Effective Long-Term Options Needed to Manage Unadoptable Wild Horses
DOI OIG: Investigative Report of Bureau of Land Management Wild Horse Buyer

WHICH CAME FIRST, THE CHICKEN OR THE EGG?

QUICK STATS

- ✘ **CONFERENCE:** Spending
- ✘ **TEAM:** National Science Foundation
- ◯ **FUMBLE:** $406,419 for a political polarization grant
- ◯ **HOW TO RECOVER THE BALL:** Redirect political science funds toward studies of higher economic and national security merit

A lot of ink has been spilled to explore the link between political polarization and the media.[98] Thanks to NSF, American tax dollars now join the plight. NSF will provide at least $406,419 to MIT researchers to attempt to answer the question, "Does media choice cause polarization or does polarization cause media choice?"[99]

It is an existential question that will be a surefire conversation-starter at any family dinner, but it is doubtful the substance of the question merits the use of hundreds of thousands of taxpayer dollars to advance the knowledge of whether MSNBC and Fox News are the cause or result of the American political system. If the government study does confirm a linkage, will the response be to limit the First Amendment right to a free press?

NSF is supposed to advance transformative research, specifically "the pursuit of national policies for the promotion of basic research and education in the sciences and engineering."[100] NSF should stick to that pursuit and reserve the questions of political persuasion for think tanks and other disinterested bodies. Polarization has become an increasing and challenging feature of American politics. Perhaps there will be a temporary thaw in the polarization to unite against such frivolous spending of tax dollars.

RECOVERY

NSF reports that it is only able to fund a fraction of the 50,000 research proposals it receives every year.[101] NSF undertakes brilliant research that benefits all American families. Congress should make sure taxpayer dollars are directed toward transformative research. Leave existential political persuasion questions to the talking heads.

For more information, please visit:
Pew Research Center: Political Polarization & Media Habits
NSF: Collaborative Research: A New Design for Identifying Persuasion Effects and Selection in Media Exposure Experiments via Patient Preference Trials

CASINOS COULD HIT JACKPOT FROM TAXPAYER-FUNDED RESEARCH

QUICK STATS

- ✗ **CONFERENCE:** Spending
- ✗ **TEAM:** National Science Foundation
- ○ **FUMBLE:** $50,000 for random casino numbers
- ○ **HOW TO RECOVER THE BALL:** Congress should work with NSF to ensure grants are not provided to advance research that private industries can complete

If random is the goal, NSF has a grant for that. Last year, NSF awarded $50,000 to the University of Michigan to create a technology that "exploits a new solution space, and represents one of the first concrete applications of quantum information science, and has the potential to draw even more public interest to the field."[102] (Go ahead. Google those terms, and come back.) The ultimate goal of the program is to achieve "a certifiable random number generator based on quantum physics. The team can design an apparatus that will generate random bits while at the same time certifying that the bits are random—even without any trust in the apparatus used."[103] The award announcement cites "companies that manage electronic transactions and gambling casinos" as two potential businesses that may benefit from this research.

No one questions the importance of investing in digital security in this age. However, Americans should call into question the need to spend federal taxpayer dollars on a project the private sector is more than capable of developing on its own.

RECOVERY

NSF conducts areas of research that benefit all American families, which should be encouraged. However, Congress should work with NSF to ensure grants are not provided to advance research benefiting private industries that are capable of doing the research on their own. Banks and casinos, which would benefit from this research, are more than capable of funding it without federal assistance. American families should not be expected to pick up the tab.

For more information, please visit:
Grantome: I-Corps: Practical and Provably Secure Random Number Generator
NSF: I-Corps: Practical and Provably Secure Random Number Generator

LEATHERNECK LEFTOVERS

QUICK STATS

- ✗ **CONFERENCE:** Spending
- ✗ **TEAM:** Department of Defense
- ○ **FUMBLE:** $36 million for an empty command center
- ○ **HOW TO RECOVER THE BALL**: Require DOD to submit reports on all completed facility construction at the one-, three-, and five-year marks to certify the facility's use compared to the original construction justification

In January 2010 DOD requested $36 million to construct a 64,000 square-foot command and control facility at Camp Leatherneck in the Helmand Province of Afghanistan. For perspective a football field including end zones is only 57,600 square feet. After awarding, designing, and building the entire project, The Special Inspector General for Afghanistan Reconstruction (SIGAR) found in 2013 the facility was unused and obviously unnecessary.[civ]

The SIGAR investigation found written evidence that subordinate commanders questioned the requirement for the facility but were later overruled. In the end SIGAR offered six process-improvement recommendations that included holding the decision-makers accountable. DOD only agreed with one of the recommendations (and partially agreed with two others) but chose not to hold anyone accountable. In 2014 the U.S. officially transferred Camp Leatherneck (including its $36 million command and control facility) back to Afghan control.

RECOVERY

The men and women of America's armed services have fought, bled, and died to protect freedom. If there is a resource they need to better do their job, they should have it. However, DOD should do a better job of ensuring it spends money on resources to actually help troops, not just create big empty buildings. Spending money on useless projects does not make the U.S. safer, and it is unclear how it advances American interests in Afghanistan. Congress should require DOD to submit reports on all facility construction at one-, three-, and five-year increments to certify the facility's use compared to the original construction justification. Knowing these reports will be required will cause DOD to ensure the long-term planning for facility use is complete before construction begins.

For more information, please visit:
SIGAR: $36 Million Command and Control Facility at Camp Leatherneck, Afghanistan: Unwanted, unneeded, and unused
Army Times: Report slams Army officers over unused $36M facility

$30,000 FOR A BEETLE?
(NOT THE VOLKSWAGEN KIND)

QUICK STATS

- ✗ **CONFERENCE:** Spending
- ✗ **TEAM:** Fish and Wildlife Service
- ◯ **FUMBLE:** $30,000 for American Burying Beetle credits
- ◯ **HOW TO RECOVER THE BALL:** Remove the American Burying Beetle from the endangered species list to avoid unnecessary spending on efforts to protect their habitat

For most Americans $30,000 is a substantial amount of money that could pay off debt, purchase a vehicle, or maybe even buy a home. What about $30,000 to secure a house for a bug? That is the price some must pay in "beetle credits" to have access to land without disturbing the habitat of the American Burying Beetle, an insect that teeters on being listed as endangered by the federal government. The American Burying Beetle was listed as an endangered species in 1989 as part of the Endangered Species Act.[105] Across the country its numbers have soared, yet the beetle still remains listed as threatened by FWS. Companies within the oil and gas industry have been known to pay upward of $30,000 per drilling well in "beetle credits" to gain access to and develop land on which the beetle may reside.[106] Remember, the companies who pay for these beetle credits pass that cost on to you, the American consumer.

The federal government has an obligation to serve as a steward of U.S. land and maintain the habitat for God's creatures, but is spending that much really necessary for an insect that no longer needs such protection? Surely not. Currently FWS has approved the Industry Conservation Plan to permit projects in the beetle's habitat for the next year. This is a good first step to remove the beetle as a hindrance to further economic development. However, removing the beetle from the list of endangered species would bring long-term stability and predictability to those looking to expand oil and gas activities or develop land. The population of the beetle continues to soar, but now FWS is focused on the "habitat" protection of the insect. Bugs should never get priority protection over people. Americans should hope termites and ants are never labeled "threatened" by FWS.

Photo: Cincinnati Zoo

RECOVERY
To prevent such a deterrent for construction and to save American consumers from having the costs transferred to them, the American Burying Beetle should be removed from the list of endangered species. While beetle populations continue to increase across the Midwest, it is apparent the beetle lacks the primary criteria for remaining on the list, and Congress should remove it. In the short term, FWS should continue with its plan to permit projects in the beetle's habitat until the list of endangered species receives an update.

For more information, please visit:
U.S. Fish & Wildlife Service: American Burying Beetle Impact Assessment for Project Reviews
Osages You Need To Know: Our Beloved American Burying Beetle

PROMISES NOT KEPT

QUICK STATS

- ✘ **CONFERENCE:** Spending
- ✘ **TEAM:** Department of the Interior
- ○ **FUMBLE:** Failure to adequately meet trust responsibilities to Indians
- ○ **RECOVERY:** Through in-depth consultation with Tribes and American Indians, Congress should ensure federal trust responsibilities are met

Through the signing of treaties in the early 1800s and numerous commitments made over the last 100 years, the federal government has many trust responsibilities to Tribes and American Indians. From education, to health care, to economic development, countless federal programs and funding opportunities exist for Tribes and individual American Indians. Indeed, according to DOI, the entire federal government spent $19.329 billion on programs impacting Indians just this year.[107]

The problem is the federal government fails to ensure federal programs for Indians actually make a difference, often placing a premium on quantity over quality. Programs are also divided, and many are duplicative with little to no coordination between DOI's BIA and every other cabinet-level department. Education programs for Indians are provided through DOI's BIE, DOEd, and HHS's housing programs are divided between BIA and HUD. Job programs for Indians are found within both BIA and the DOL. Funding for justice programs can be obtained from the BIA, DOJ, and even HUD. It is a convoluted mess with no coordination and in many cases very little oversight of program management or real evaluation for effectiveness.

The U.S. has an undeniable obligation to American Indians, and no one in the federal government can definitively say the federal government meets that obligation. It is easy to throw more money at a problem, create new programs, and claim success. It is quite another matter to actually fix the problem. Here are a few examples of inefficient use of federal taxpayer dollars through mismanagement and duplication:

Education
BIE within DOI has an FY 2015 budget of $810.531 million.[108] BIE is responsible for the funding of 183 elementary and secondary schools, 54 of which are directly operated by BIE.[109] BIE also operates two post-secondary institutions. All of the schools are on or near Tribal reservations. To be clear: BIE does focus almost exclusively on students who are not in a public school system. The only exception is the Johnson O'Malley program, which provides funding for Indian students in public schools.[110]

At the same time, DOEd, the federal department *actually tasked* with ensuring Americans have education opportunities, also has responsibilities to Indians. Of DOEd's FY 2015 budget, $123.939 million goes to Indian children in schools—either public schools or BIE schools.[111] In fact 24 percent of BIE funding for BIE-operated schools actually comes from the DOEd.[112] HHS also has an education program focused on funding for Tribal language preservation. This year the program provided $4.054 million in three-year grants to provide language preservation education.[113]

GAO recently released a report showing that while BIE schools spend 56 percent more per pupil than the average public school, its students are still in dilapidated schools, teachers are underpaid, and students are not given many opportunities for success.[114] GAO also points out that BIE lacks the trained staff to properly administor schools.[115] Indeed, BIE has struggled to even construct a bus barn correctly. BIE funded a $1.5 million bus barn in South Dakota, but while a bus is serviced on the hydraulic lift, the doors cannot shut because the barn is not long enough to properly house a full-size school bus.[116]

Housing and Community Development
Anyone who has spent time on Indian reservations knows the desperate need for housing and community development. The compassion typical of reservation life helps decrease the number of homeless people in Indian Country. That compassion usually comes in the form of welcoming more and more people into homes, which leads to major overcrowding followed by HUD stepping in with a $650 million housing block grant program for Indians, usually operated by Tribes.[117] An additional $66 million is set aside for community planning and development in Indian Country.[118]

Within DOI, BIA also has an $8 million housing program and receives $2.2 million for "community development oversight."[119] Admittedly, in a country with a multi-trillion budget each year, spending $10 million is a drop in the bucket. However, this amount adds up. Having two offices in two departments work on the same issues is inefficient and is actually a disservice to American Indians.

Justice
Law enforcement matters present a unique problem on reservations. Sometimes Tribal law enforcement has jurisdiction. Sometimes the state or local police have jurisdiction, but the federal government always has jurisdiction. The federal government also has an important interest to support the continued development of Tribal police and court systems. This is why DOJ provides $30 million for Tribal law enforcement and has a $33 million grant through the COPS Hiring Program to assist with hiring and training police officers.[120] DOJ also provides $35.975 million in grants to Tribal governments to enforce the Violence Against Women Act (or VAWA), an additional $6.2 million to support the creation of non-governmental coalitions to combat violence against women on reservations, and $5 million for a Tribal youth program to combat delinquency.[121] Tribes can also utilize the funding from block grants offered by HUD or crime prevention and safety in the areas that benefit from the overall grant.[122]

BIA spends $352,850,000 in public safety and justice programs, which includes $4.7 million for an Indian police academy, $5.2 million for Tribal justice support, and $6.25 million for law enforcement program management.[123] Of that amount BIA law enforcement spends $192.8 million in areas that lack Tribal law enforcement.[124] The problem with all of this is that more than $400 million is spent between DOJ and BIA, and what is the result? Murders, sexual assaults, drugs, and other major crimes occur on a daily basis with little done to stop them. If all resources were strategically focused, more could be done.

Mismanagement of Energy Resources
Tribes throughout the U.S. have tremendous potential for energy production. Together, Tribes and individual American Indians own the third-largest mineral resources, particularly coal, gas, and oil. Tribal land can also be utilized to produce 1.1 billion megawatt-hours of electricity from wind energy and 14 billion megawatt-hours of solar energy.[125] Unfortunately the federal government often stands in the way of reaching this potential.

Earlier this year GAO released a report entitled, "Poor Management by BIA Has Hindered Energy Development on Indian Lands."[126] While acknowledging some Tribes lack the financial capacity to take advantage of resources, the report faults BIA for an inefficient and confusing system that slows down the resource exploration and development process. For instance GAO points out that those seeking permits for oil, gas, or wind energy projects could require permits from at least BIA, BLM, EPA, and FWS.[127] This is on top of the requirements found in the National Environmental Policy Act, which mandates that all federal environmental laws be followed during Tribal energy development because the land or resources are managed by the federal government and federal agencies are involved in the development process through permitting.[128]

Unfortunately BIA does not have a process to determine how long it takes to review applications and requests, but there is anecdotal evidence that the process is very lengthy. BIA reportedly took 18 months to process one wind lease, more than eight years to review right-of-way applications, and more than three years to review and approve a different wind energy project.[129]

Even if a Tribe can get through the difficult permitting process, there are other roadblocks to energy development. GAO reports that BIA lacks "the data it needs to verify ownership of some oil and gas resources, easily identify resources available for lease, or easily identify where leases are in effect."[130] This is generally because BIA has either lost the information or the information it does have is old and outdated.

Reform Needed
DOL spends $46 million on programs to assist American Indians (plus Alaska Natives and Native Hawaiians) to find jobs and job training.[131] BIA spends $11.463 million on the same thing.[132] BIA provides more than $26 million for tribal roads[133] while DOT spends $450 million on the Tribal Transportation Program.[134] Both programs support the continued construction and maintenance of roads within Indian Country. There are many, many more examples.

These programs are not necessarily wasteful, and the work they intend to accomplish is important. However, the solution to problems in Indian Country is not the creation of new programs or just additional funding. Congress, in thorough consultation with Tribal governments and all American Indians, needs to determine the best way to remove duplicative or inefficient services and ensure the U.S. meets its trust responsibilities in the best way possible. If BIA is indeed the best agency to provide all services and programs for Tribes, then other federal departments should eliminate duplicative programs, and BIA should be reformed to become truly capable of fulfilling all trust responsibilities. It is possible that each federal department, serving as experts for their respective fields, is best tasked to provide services to Tribes and individual Indians. If so, BIA should defer to these departments and take on the role of Tribal advocate. This would allow BIA to still ensure trust responsibilities are met by standing next to Tribes as they work directly with each department and agency.

No matter the best way forward, there should only be one place for assistance and funding for education of American Indian children, one place for assistance and funding for Tribal police and courts, and one place for assistance and funding for each Indian program. Congress should recognize the importance of getting this right. American Indians deserve the federal government's best effort, and right now, they are not getting it.

For more information on federal funding for tribes and American Indians, please visit:
DOI: FY2016 Federal Funding for Programs Serving tribes and Native American Communities
DOI: Budget Justifications and Performance Information Fiscal Year 2016 – Indian Affairs
HUD: Congressional Justifications FY2016
Department of Education: Indian Education Fiscal Year 2016 Budget Request
DOL: FY2016 Budget in Brief
DOJ: FY2016 DOJ Request – State, Local, and Tribal Law Enforcement Assistance
DOT: FHWA FY2016 Budget

For more information, please visit:
GAO Report: Indian Affairs: Bureau of Indian Education Needs to Improve Oversight of School Spending
GAO Testimony: Further Actions on GAO Recommendations Needed to Address Systemic Management Challenges with Indian Education
GAO Testimony: Further Actions on GAO Recommendations Needed to Address Systemic Management Challenges with Indian Education
GAO Report: Indian Energy Development: Poor Management by BIA Has Hindered Energy Development on Indian Lands
The New York Times: Higher Crime, Fewer Charges on Indian Land

ALL LIT UP!

QUICK STATS

- **CONFERENCE:** Spending
- **TEAM:** National Park Service
- **FUMBLE:** $65,473 to demonstrate what happens to bugs when the lights go out
- **HOW TO RECOVER THE BALL:** Direct NPS to be more responsible with spending; only request grant funding when national interests will be advanced

People flock out of the cities on family vacations to take in breathtaking views and enjoy quiet, wide-open spaces. People also leave the big cities because they want to get away from huge buildings and brightly lit signs that block out the sky and make it impossible to see the stars at night. This has been normal human behavior for as long as there have been cities.

Photo: Shutterstock

Soon the world will also have the chance to know how the insects feel about brightly lit cities. In 2015 NPS awarded a $65,473 grant to study the responses insects have to the placement of artificial lights and noise in areas that traditionally have had little to no light other than sunlight.[135]

The federal government spent more than $65,000 to study what happens if someone turns on a light at night in a rural area. Anyone raised in a rural area can attest that one way to attract insects is to turn on a light. This type of ridiculous spending is why American taxpayers have been saddled with a debt of approximately $19 trillion. NPS needs to put down the national credit card and walk away.

RECOVERY

Congress needs to clearly direct NPS, and all federal agencies for that matter, to be more responsible with federal spending and only spend when the national interest is advanced. Before requesting such a large grant, the NPS should utilize common-sense knowledge and perform a cost-benefit analysis of the necessity for such spending. It seems the more appropriate place to start would be to determine whether additional lighting is necessary and, if not, how that will impact future national park attendance by families, not insects.

For more information, please visit:
Grants.gov: Development and Testing LIDAR to Study Insect Responses to Light and Noise

FEDERAL BIKE TRAILS

QUICK STATS

- **CONFERENCE:** Regulation
- **TEAM:** Department of Transportation
- **FUMBLE:** Requirement to spend two percent of highway funding on non-motorized transportation infrastructure
- **HOW TO RECOVER THE BALL:** Put fewer requirements on how state transportation departments must spend infrastructure dollars

Road and bridge maintenance and construction is typically funded through a user fee system—each time Americans fill up their car's tank, 18.3 cents from the sale of every gallon of gasoline and 24.3 cents of every gallon of diesel goes into the federal highway trust fund for states to spend on the infrastructure drivers use to get home every day.[136] This system allows individuals who use the roads and bridges to pay for them to be in good condition without charging those who do not use them. Or at least that is how user fee systems work in theory. Instead the federally collected dollars in the highway trust fund are used to fund bike paths, scenic viewing areas, and the conversion of abandoned railroad routes into pedestrian paths, all while roads in many states continue to deteriorate.

This is all happening because DOT requires states to spend about two percent of their highway funding on a program called Transportation Alternatives—infrastructure for non-motorized and non-gas tax-contributing transportation infrastructure.[137] This two percent is not an insignificant amount of money. In 2015 two percent of each state's combined allotment amounted to about $820 million.[138] By comparison, the massive undertaking of the I-40 Crosstown reconstruction, a multi-year project that updated a four-mile stretch of I-40 in Oklahoma City from a three-lane highway built to carry 76,000 vehicles daily to a five-lane highway that could handle up to 173,000 vehicles daily, clocked in at about $680 million.[139] Without these federal requirements, states could be empowered to take on more multi-year, significant projects that help shorten the commutes of thousands of people and ease the movement of goods through the vast economy.

RECOVERY

The process to determine which projects are the federal government's responsibility and how Americans can cover those costs is in need of reform to be sustainable into the future. Over the past few years, the highway trust fund has needed an influx of general revenue funding to continue to pay for road projects that are authorized under the law.[140] However, the federal government can implement small changes to make it easier for states to patch potholes and build bridges. Not requiring them to use highway money meant for roads to build bike paths would be a start. The next step is to stop the constant expansion of the federal highway inventory. More miles of road are added each year to the interstate system; the U.S. cannot continue to expand the federal footprint with the same amount of money.

For more information, please visit:
Federal Highway Authority: Transportation Alternatives Program (TAP)
Oklahoma DOT: I-40 Crosstown
CRS Report: The Federal Excise Tax on Motor Fuels and the Highway Trust Fund: Current Law and Legislative History

FUNDING FOR PHANTOM FUELS

QUICK STATS

- ✗ **CONFERENCE:** Spending
- ✗ **TEAM:** Internal Revenue Service
- ⭕ **FUMBLE:** Billions of dollars in tax credits for non-existent biofuels
- ⭕ **HOW TO RECOVER THE BALL:** Eliminate the incentive for a fuel the market cannot provide

Congress has a knack for mandating the use of certain goods by consumers and then subsidizing their production. This is precisely what the government does with the production tax credit for cellulosic biofuels, which are additives blended into the U.S. gasoline supply in the name of lowering dependence on foreign oil. Since 2009 biofuels made from switchgrass and similar feedstocks received a $1.01 per gallon tax credit.[141]

Not only is this subsidy expensive, it is highly ineffective. For 2015, the RFS requires that three billion gallons of cellulosic biofuels be blended into the gasoline supply.[142] But there is a huge problem; all American manufacturers of cellulosic biofuels combined only produced around 100 million gallon, far less than the required three billion gallons. In other words the tax credit is unsuccessful at creating the necessary supply to meet the demand created by Congress. EPA finds itself mandating that Americans use a fuel that does not exist, even when Congress forced taxpayers to pay for it.

RECOVERY

Despite the significant financial incentive, which amounts to $55 million each time Congress enacts a two-year extension of the credit,[143] the goal of spurring technological advancement in the area of cellulosic biofuel is simply not working. Congress should eliminate the costly and ineffective mandate. American families can understand their government working to decrease its reliance on foreign oil and save them money. But the biofuels tax credit does neither. Congress cannot pay for a fuel that does not exist.

For more information, please visit:
EPA: Renewable Fuel Standard Program
United States Senate Finance Committee: Provisions in the Chairman's Mark: EXPIRE Act
CRS Report: Renewable Fuel Standard (RFS): Overview and Issues
CRS Report: The Renewable Fuel Standard (RFS): Cellulosic Biofuels

LAW VS. EXECUTIVE ORDERS

QUICK STATS

- ✗ **CONFERENCE:** Regulation
- ✗ **TEAM:** Government-wide
- ○ **FUMBLE:** Accountability by Executive Order, not by law
- ○ **HOW TO RECOVER THE BALL:** Enhance agency accountability by codifying Executive Orders 12866 and 13563

Regulations issued by executive agencies should be tools used to implement laws passed by Congress. The Legislative Branch creates the laws, and the Executive Branch implements them. However, because the legislative process is often cumbersome and difficult (even though that is how the Founders intended it), the regulatory process can be used by the Executive Branch to advance regulatory policies beyond those that Congress likely intended. This can result in oppressive or excessive regulations that hurt farmers, small businesses, and everyday Americans—without due process to individuals who are affected.

Executive Orders 12866 and 13563, signed by Presidents Clinton and Obama, require significant regulatory actions to be submitted to the Office of Information and Regulatory Affairs, part of OMB, for review.[144] Under these Executive Orders, federal agencies are required to do their due diligence before imposing more regulations on Americans—such as assessing the costs and benefits of proposed rules and regulations and considering possible alternatives. They are also directed to coordinate their regulatory activities and seek the views of individuals likely to be affected by the rulemaking.[145] Transparency provisions allow the American people, Congress, and interested parties to contribute to the rulemaking process.

RECOVERY

Analytical requirements for regulations should be written into law, passed by Congress, and not left only as Executive Orders that can be withdrawn at any time without congressional approval. Congressional action in this area would provide the basis for judicial review of an agency's compliance with the law and would serve as a reminder to the Executive that Congress has a role to play in federal rules. This would give businesses and agencies an additional layer of guaranteed stability and consistency. Congress, exercising its constitutionally provided oversight role, could also remind agencies that they need to stop issuing burdensome and costly regulations that hurt American businesses and families.

For more information, please visit:
EPA: Summary of Executive Order 12866 – Regulatory Planning and Review
Federal Register Archives: Executive Order 12866
Federal Register: Executive Order 13563

GOT A PERMIT FOR THAT?

QUICK STATS

- ✗ **CONFERENCE:** Regulation
- ✗ **TEAM:** Army Corps of Engineers and other agencies
- ◯ **FUMBLE:** Duplicative, costly federal permits
- ◯ **HOW TO RECOVER THE BALL:** Pass the Federal Permitting Improvement Act

America's mining operations face ever-growing duplicative permitting requirements that prevent them from selling their products like Northern White sand, which is necessary for natural gas extraction at home and abroad. In March 2015 the U.S. Senate Subcommittee on Regulatory Affairs and Federal Management held a hearing focused on the federal regulatory process at which former Office of Information and Regulatory Affairs Administrator John D. Graham testified on the permitting difficulties sand miners face.

In his testimony Mr. Graham stated that in order to maintain sand mining operations, companies in Wisconsin and Minnesota must secure 15 permits from local and state authorities in addition to federal permits from USACE required by the Clean Water, Clean Air, and Endangered Species Acts. Illustrating how confusing and duplicative permitting requirements harm small businesses, Mr. Graham testified that only large mining companies can afford the "team of lawyers, engineers, and scientists" necessary to navigate the permitting process.[146]

These duplicative and costly permitting requirements will force American companies to relocate their operations and the jobs they provide to other countries, which would have a massive impact on the communities that rely on mining jobs. Many countries' environmental regulations are not as strong as those in the U.S., and by forcing American mining jobs to move overseas, U.S. permitting requirements will harm both the environment and American families.

RECOVERY

The U.S. can start to streamline the process by sending the Federal Permitting Improvement Act of 2015 to the President's desk.[147] This bipartisan bill would improve the permitting process and ease duplicative regulatory burdens by requiring greater transparency, earlier public participation, and increased interagency coordination. The federal government must work to ensure that federal regulations do not cause Americans to lose their jobs.

For more information, please visit:
United States Senate Committee on Homeland Security and Governmental Affairs: Examining Federal Rulemaking Challenges and Areas of Improvement Within the Existing Regulatory Process
S.280 – Federal Permitting Improvement Act of 2015

USAID: BLAME THE AFGHANS, NOT US

QUICK STATS

- ✗ **CONFERENCE:** Spending
- ✗ **TEAM:** Agency for International Development
- ○ **FUMBLE:** $7.7 million for an industrial park
- ○ **HOW TO RECOVER THE BALL:** Require federal agencies to monitor spending projects to ensure they have the desired effect

In July 2008 USAID completed the Gorimor Industrial Park at a cost of $7.7 million and turned it over to the Afghanistan Investment Support Agency (AISA). The industrial park in Balkh Province, Afghanistan, was built to create more than 900 local jobs, but six years later only two business and 22 individuals work at the site. In 2014 the SIGAR inspected the site to determine why the Gorimar Industrial Park was not utilized.

The underutilization was intially blamed on the lack of electricity and water. But when SIGAR requested contract files to assess whether the contractor met contract requirements to provide electricity and water, USAID was unable to produce them—despite a federal requirement that agencies keep contracts greater than $2,000 for six years and three months after final payment. Absent other evidence from USAID, it would seem they failed to properly document and retain contracts. By the time the inspection ended, USAID blamed AISA for its inability to manage the park.[148]

Photo: SIGAR

RECOVERY

It is reasonable for hard-working American taxpayers to expect their government to properly spend money. Congress must do better to exercise its oversight responsibilities to ensure that USAID and all federal agencies utilize tax dollars responsibly. Congress should require USAID to put in place reasonable guideposts to measure the success of all spending projects. This would include monitoring support and economic development grants to ensure that the funds have had the desired effect.

For more information, please visit:
SIGAR: Gorimar Industrial Park: Lack of Electricity and Water Have Left This $7.7 Million U.S.-funded Industrial Park Underutilized by Afghan Businesses
Foreign Policy: Afghan Watchdog Finds That If You Build It, They Won't Necessarily Come

VA: RETURN ON SOLAR INVESTMENT IN JUST 38.59 YEARS!

QUICK STATS

- ✘ **CONFERENCE:** Spending
- ✘ **TEAM:** Department of Veterans Affairs
- ◯ **FUMBLE:** $8 million VA solar boondoggle
- ◯ **HOW TO RECOVER THE BALL:** For spending on infrastructure projects, the return on investment should be less than ten years

The VA facility in Little Rock, AR, moved never-used solar panels to new heights—on top of a parking structure. In April 2015 only two years after completion and at a cost of $8 million[149] from a federal government grant, the hostpial tore down its never-used solar panels. The 1,400 inactive solar panels were taken down to make room for a new parking garage that was approved after the solar panels were installed.[150]

If that is not bad enough, in response to this issue, the VA assured Congress taxpayers will save $207,266 annually once the never-used panels in Little Rock are activated, which means that in about 38 ½ years, American taxpayers will start to get a return on their investment.[151] No American family would ever buy solar panels for their own home if the return on investment was greater than a mortgage, so why should VA?

RECOVERY

It is admirable for agencies to look for ways to save money in the long run, a responsible budget practice that families do on a daily basis. But no family would invest in a cost-saving measure that kicks in after a generation. Congress should ensure that all federal spending for buildings and facilities is cost effective and immediately beneficial.

For more information, please visit:
VA Letters to Congressman French Hill
Hot Springs Daily: Little Rock VA Throws Away $8,000,000 But Doesn't Pay Arkansas Hospitals For Care

DOCTOR UNCLE SAM

QUICK STATS

- ✘ **CONFERENCE:** Spending
- ✘ **TEAM:** Department of Defense
- ◯ **FUMBLE:** $25 million
- ◯ **HOW TO RECOVER THE BALL:** DOD's medical research should focus on injuries or illnesses directly related to defense activities

According to NCI, approximately 230,000 new cases of breast cancer are diagnosed annually.[152] The number is more than a statistic; most American families have someone who has fought breast cancer or know someone who has. It is the second-most common type of cancer in the world and the most common cancer for women. It is beyond time to find a cure and NCI and NIH should lead the way. There is certainly a national interest in funding cancer research, but the federal government should funnel those dollars to a targeted number of agencies who can continually build on their cutting-edge developments, rather than spread a finite number of dollars around a wide variety of entities.

In August 2015 DOD offered a $25 million grant "to support promising research that has high potential to lead to or make breakthroughs in breast cancer."[153] No preliminary data is required, according to the grant solicitation. DOD looks for innovative, high-risk, high-reward research in the earliest stages of idea development.[154] When federal institutions already do the same thing, this $25 million could either go toward much-needed defense capabilities or could be transferred to another entity already working on breast cancer research.

RECOVERY

This is a admirable goal, but not for DOD, which should instead focus on national security. Any federal dollars going toward cancer research should flow from NCI or NIH, the natural place for medical research. Congress should work with DOD to ensure any medical research it conducts is directly related to injuries or illnesses occurring in defense-related activities.

For more information, please visit:
Grants.gov: DOD Breast Cancer Breakthrough Award Levels 1 and 2

LIFELINE PHONE PROGRAM

QUICK STATS

- ✗ **CONFERENCE:** Spending
- ✗ **TEAM:** Federal Communications Commission
- ○ **FUMBLE:** Failure to ensure program requirements meet population and geographic realities
- ○ **HOW TO RECOVER THE BALL:** Implement stricter requirements and oversight for subsidy qualifications

FCC's Lifeline program began in 1985 to provide discounted telephone service to low-income families—particularly those in hard-to-reach areas with little access to emergency landline telephone services. In 2005 the service was extended to encompass pre-paid cell phone plans in addition to landline service. FCC requirements dictate qualified individuals must meet income requirements at or below 135 percent of the federal poverty guidelines or participate in specific federal assistance programs to qualify for the program.[155]

Lifeline is funded through a service fee (meaning a tax) called the Universal Service Fund, which is on every American's phone bill. In 2014 $1.6 billion was allocated for the Lifeline program to serve its more than 12 million users.[156] The majority of beneficiaries receive a monthly $9.25 discount subsidy toward their telephone service cost. However, due to low telephone availability on Tribal lands, qualified residences receive an additional $25 subsidy, which brings the total monthly subsidy to $34.25.[157]

Since 2005 the Lifeline program has been riddled with waste, fraud, and abuse. One of the largest areas of waste is in Oklahoma due to FCC's broad parameters for Tribal land boundaries. Historically, FCC classified most of Oklahoma as Tribal land, which means all but 451 of the state's 265,961 Lifeline recipients qualify for more than $400 each in Tribal subsidies annually, though most of the recipients are not Tribal members.[158] As a result, Oklahoma receives the second-largest allocation of Lifeline funds, which total more than $128 million.[159] Oklahoma accounts for more than half of the 417,000 Tribal subsidy recipients in the nation.[160]

The Tribal Lifeline subsidy was originally intended to provide discounted telephone service to low-income Tribal members who lived on Tribal land and need an emergency telephone. In June 2015 FCC updated the Oklahoma Tribal maps to slightly narrow the geographical scope of qualified territory.[161] While this is a small step in the right direction, to fully address the problem we should move towards needs-based Tribal designations.

RECOVERY

The Commission should clearly define Tribal membership and designated underserved areas. Individuals who seek the Tribal subsidy should provide proof of Tribal citizenship/membership or residency in designated underserved areas within Tribal boundaries. The additional aid should be reserved for the truly underserved

For more information, please visit:
USAC: 2014 Annual Report
USAC: 2015 FCC Filings
USAC: Lifeline Subscribers by State or Jurisdiction
National Review: What Those Rising Taxes on Your Phone Bill Pay For: A Fraud-Friendly 'Obamaphone' Program

SUBSIDIZED SPORT STADIUMS

QUICK STATS

- ✗ **CONFERENCE:** Spending
- ✗ **TEAM:** Internal Revenue Service
- ○ **FUMBLE:** $542 million over the next ten years for tax-exempt bonds subsidizing private enterprise
- ○ **HOW TO RECOVER THE BALL:** Congress should act to make stadiums ineligible for use of tax-free municipal bonds and stop subsidizing multi-million dollar franchises

For the past twenty years, publicly subsidized stadiums have become an increasingly popular means for areas to attract and retain professional teams. The tax-exempt federal bonds primarily used to subsidize the privately owned franchises cost the taxpayers millions of dollars annually, with most of the benefits accumulating to a select few.[162] Projections from the U.S. Treasury estimate that eliminating the tax exemption could save the federal government approximately $542 million over the next ten years.[163]

According to a study by Bloomberg Business, "Over the life of the $17 billion of exempt debt issued to build stadiums since 1986, the last of which matures in 2047, taxpayer subsidies to bondholders will total $4 billion."[164]

RECOVERY

Public funding should be focused on broader projects that not only benefit a larger population, but also serve a more tangible public policy purpose. Congress should act to make stadiums ineligible for use of tax-free municipal bonds and stop subsidizing multi-million dollar franchises.

For more information, please visit:
Department of the Treasury: General Explanations of the Administration's Fiscal Year 2016 Revenue Proposals
GAO: Tax Policy: Tax-Exempt Status of Certain Bonds Merits Reconsideration, and Apparent Noncompliance with Issuance Cost Limitations Should Be Addressed
Bloomberg Business: In Stadium Building Spree, U.S. Taxpayers Lose $4 Billion

UNFUNDED MANDATES TO CITIES, TRIBES, STATES, AND PRIVATE BUSINESSES

QUICK STATS

- ✗ **CONFERENCE:** Regulation
- ✗ **TEAM:** Government-wide
- ○ **FUMBLE:** Burdensome mandates on governments and private entities
- ○ **HOW TO RECOVER THE BALL:** Create a more transparent process for congressional consideration of legislation and agency rulemaking through the passage of the Unfunded Mandates Information and Transparency Act

It is safe to say that most Americans believe Washington is out of touch. Executive agencies and Congress have become far too comfortable forcing laws and regulations on state, local, and Tribal entities and private businesses without bothering to figure out the costs others will take on to carry out the imposing instructions from Washington. These laws and rules, known as unfunded mandates, not only stealthily conceal the true cost of implementation, but they also place undue burdens on smaller entities that must comply with the law but do not have the pool of financial resources available to the federal government.

Between 1996 and 2014, CBO identified 141 private-sector mandates that will cost more than $100 million in compliance. During this same time period, Congress enacted 18 new inter-governmental mandates that cost at least $50 million for compliance of state and local governments.[165] Examples of such costly unfunded mandates include $13.3 million annually in administrative costs for local schools to comply with federal school lunch regulations and $1.46 billion for automakers to comply with federal fuel efficiency standards.[166] These expensive mandates inevitably impact American families who have to spend more money on goods and services from the regulated business and pay higher taxes to make up for their local government compliance costs.

The problem of unfunded mandates dictated from Washington, DC, is not new. In fact the Unfunded Mandates Reform Act (UMRA) of 1995 was passed to provide a tool for Congress to examine the unfunded cost implications of potential legislation prior to passage and to require executive agencies to assess unfunded mandates during the rulemaking process.

However, the law is plagued with loopholes. For example, a large flaw with the UMRA process is that it does not apply to regulations promulgated by independent regulatory agencies like the National Labor Relations Board, which acts independently of presidential authority. It also does not apply to regulations that are published without a general notice of proposed rulemaking. A GAO report found that about half of all final major rules in a two-year span were finalized without an UMRA analysis of these gaps, even though the rules had "impacts on nonfederal parties that those affected might perceive as unfunded mandates."[167]

RECOVERY

The Unfunded Mandates Information and Transparency Act of 2015, introduced earlier this year by Senator Deb Fischer (NE) in the U.S. Senate and Rep. Virginia Foxx (NC) in the House, seeks to build on previous legislation to hold the federal government accountable for the mandates it imposes.[168] Congress should quickly pass this bill to protect American families from the higher costs and taxes as states, counties, cities, Tribes, and businesses enforce the unfunded mandates.

For more information visit:
CBO: A Review of CBO's Activities in 2014 Under the Unfunded Mandates Reform Act
Senators Lankford and Fischer Introduce Bill to Bring Transparency to Unfunded Mandates

INTERNATIONAL MARINE TURTLES OF MYSTERY

QUICK STATS

- ✗ **CONFERENCE:** Spending
- ✗ **TEAM:** Environmental Protection Agency
- ○ **FUMBLE:** $59 million spent over four years on international conservation
- ○ **HOW TO RECOVER THE BALL:** Leverage private efforts, where they exist, on conservation, instead of investing taxpayer dollars

Using tax dollars collected from hard-working American families, the federal government made its species conservation efforts international.

Beginning in 1988, the federal government created several international species conservation funds to provide technical assistance for species conservation, law enforcement, and habitat conservation, for species including elephants, great apes, and marine turtles.[169] All of these efforts cost American taxpayers millions of dollars. In the last two years alone, the federal government has put over $18 million toward these programs.[170]

RECOVERY

Responsible species conservation and stewardship of the land is an admirable and accomplishable goal. However, the fund received nearly $89 million from private partners from 2008-2012.[171] Congress should stop funding this international conservation program, which is more than capable of raising funds on its own. An admirable goal does not make it a national interest. With an almost $19 trillion national debt, this program cannot be justified.

For more information on Multinational Species Conservation Agreements, please visit:
U.S. Fish & Wildlife Service: Multinational Species Conservation Acts
CRS Report: International Species Conservation Funds

ONE OF THESE ENTITLEMENTS IS NOT LIKE THE OTHER

QUICK STATS

- **CONFERENCE:** Spending
- **TEAM:** Social Security Administration
- **FUMBLE:** $5.7 billion
- **HOW TO RECOVER THE BALL:** Pass H.R. 918, the Social Security Disability Insurance and Unemployment Benefits Double Dip Elimination Act of 2015

For some reason the federal government treats certain entitlement programs (SSDI, UI, and TAA) the same. UI is for jobless workers who seek re-employment. TAA provides federally funded benefits to workers who lost their jobs due to trade and who have also exhausted their UI benefits. SSDI, on the other hand, is only for individuals who cannot perform substantial work because of a medical impairment that is expected to last for at least a year.

SSDI benefits should be for those who truly cannot work, not for people who can work and therefore qualify for TAA or UI. However, in FY 2010 at least 117,000 people received SSDI and UI benefits simultaneously.[172] In other words one part of the federal government considered them medically impaired and unable to work while another considered them to be temporarily unemployed and looking for a job. GAO estimates the overlapping cash benefits paid to these recipients totaled more than $281 million from DI and more than $575 million from UI.[173]

RECOVERY

There are many ways to fix this problem. One way is for Congress to eliminate the concurrent benefit of SSDI and UI payments, which would save $2 billion over ten years.[174] If the concurrent receipt of SSDI, UI, and TAA was eliminated, the savings would be $5.7 billion over ten years.[175] President Obama suggested reducing the SSDI benefit in any month that UI benefits are also received to eliminate the duplicate payment. The estimated ten-year savings of the President's proposal are just over $2 billion.[176] Congress should analyze all of these plans and select a way forward that eliminates duplication and saves taxpayer money.

For more information, please visit:
House of Representatives Committee on Ways and Means: Social Security Disability Insurance and Unemployment Benefits Double Dip Elimination Act of 2015
GPO: S. 499 The Social Security Disability Insurance and Unemployment Benefits Double Dip Elimination Act of 2015

EPA POWER GRAB: FINAL "WATERS OF THE UNITED STATES" RULE

QUICK STATS

- ✘ **CONFERENCE:** Regulation
- ✘ **TEAM:** Environmental Protection Agency
- ○ **FUMBLE:** $500 million per year in costs to businesses and federal intrusion in private water and land rights
- ○ **HOW TO RECOVER THE BALL:** Federal Water Quality Protection Act; Congressional Review Act resolution of disapproval; funding limitation in FY 2016 Appropriations Bill

Photo: Shutterstock

Since the Clean Water Act was signed into law in 1972, EPA has defined and regulated America's navigable waters, which are waters "that are subject to the ebb and flow of the tide and/or are presently used, or have been used in the past, or may be susceptible for use to transport interstate or foreign commerce."[177]

When EPA and USACE finalized the "Waters of the U.S." (WOTUS) rule on August 28, 2015, they blew the former definition out of the water. The new rule expands the definition into tributaries and small rivers, which were previously regulated and protected by state governments, and expands the amount of waters that require a site-specific "jurisdictional" determination.[178] The result is more federal involvement in land-use decisions and a lessened ability to know whether a specific project requires a federal permit.

Most Americans can agree that protecting natural resources and water sources is important. When it comes to navigable waters that support interstate commerce, it is even a constitutional and national responsibility. But when the agency in charge of administering the regulation describes the rule as "contradict[ory to] long-standing and well established legal principles" in an internal memo, it should be a reminder that even EPA cannot create policies that fall outside of the jurisdiction Congress gave it.[179]

An expansive definition could mean expensive changes for anyone using the land for farming, energy exploration, and building roads and bridges. The farming community could see the need for additional permits to carry out activities that they have done for years, like fertilizing fields or putting in fences, if these activities are done near ditches deemed navigable waters—or risk being fined thousands of dollars for each day they are in "violation."[180] This only increases the cost of goods for American families and with little to show for it but paperwork.

State and local governments have protected local water sources for years. Because they are closer to the source, these government entities know how to do it best. Immediately after the rule's final issuance, 27 states stood up to assert their authority by suing EPA and USACE. A federal court then placed a temporary block on regulation enforcement, noting the burden the rule placed on state and private entities. In addition the court noted serious concerns about whether the rule exceeds EPA's jurisdiction, as previously articulated by the Supreme Court. The court also echoed USACE criticisms of the process by which changes to the rule were adopted during the rulemaking process, including whether EPA supported its policy choices with sufficient science. EPA should not disregard the limits of its own authority in the rulemaking process and issue such a rule that is unsubstantiated by both science and necessity.

RECOVERY

On April 30, 2015, Senator John Barrasso (WY) introduced a bipartisan bill to require EPA and USACE to rewrite the burdensome WOTUS rule.[181] Unfortunately a majority of Senate Democrats ultimately blocked the bill. Senator Joni Ernst's (IA) joint resolution of congressional disapproval of the WOTUS rule did successfully pass the U.S. Senate on November 4, 2015.[182] This joint resolution would roll back EPA's WOTUS rule and prevent the federal government from taking control of what it broadly defines as "navigable waterways." Congress should also consider preventing EPA and USACE from implementing this rule with funding limitations in the appropriate FY 2016 appropriations legislation. EPA should restart its rulemaking on this issue and reach out for valuable input from all Americans—rural farmers to small business owners.

For more information, please visit:
Federal Register: Clean Water Rule: Definition of "Waters of the United States"; Final Rule
S.J.Res.22
US Court of Appeals: Sixth Circuit Opinion
Army Corps of Engineers: Waters of the US Memos

ORGANIZING AROUND THE WORLD: UNIONS FOR ALL

QUICK STATS

- ✘ **CONFERENCE:** Spending
- ✘ **TEAM:** U.S. Agency for International Development
- ○ **FUMBLE:** $37.5 million
- ○ **RECOVERY:** USAID should support programs that advance national interests

USAID posted a grant notice this year in an effort to seek applications from all eligible organizations for a program that can demonstrate clear, measurable, and meaningful medium-term results and progress toward a long-term impact to increase the capacity of labor organizations (trade unions and civil society organizations); to promote workers' representation in policy processes; improve access to justice; advance the effective worldwide application of core international labor standards; and improve the welfare and livelihood opportunities of workers and their families and communities.[183]

This government-speak could be translated simply as: USAID wants to spend $37.5 million to promote labor unions around the world with "medium-term results" and "long-term impact."[184] USAID has had this mission, advanced through its Global Labor Program since 1961.[185]

RECOVERY

Every individual is free to promote the ideas and values in which he or she believes, but it is far from the federal government's responsibility to spend millions of dollars to build the capacity of labor unions in other countries. This a job better left to international labor organizations.

For more information, please visit:
Grants.gov: Global Labor Program
USAID

GOING GREEN, MOROCCAN STYLE

QUICK STATS

- ✗ **CONFERENCE:** Spending
- ✗ **TEAM:** Department of State
- ○ **FUMBLE:** $250,000 to Moroccan biodiversity
- ○ **HOW TO RECOVER THE BALL:** Establish legislative restrictions to the types of grants federal agencies can fund so appropriations benefit the American interest

The evolution of the green movement in the last ten years has impacted almost every American family. A trip to the local store offers a multitude of choices in products for consumers, whether they are green, organic, sustainable, etc. However, in the last several years, the movement became fashionable throughout the nation and the world, and now American tax dollars are used to encourage green policies in other countries.

Earlier this year State offered a $250,000 grant to kick-start the green movement in Morocco.[186] Yes, Morocco. The Administration promised to promote green growth and green jobs to help enhance biodiversity conservation in Morocco and improve management of ecologically important ecosystems. The U.S. and Morocco signed a Joint Statement on Environmental Cooperation in 2006. The 2014-2017 Plan of Action reflects current priorities for trade-related environmental activities.[187] The Administration's failures involving "green" ventures domestically and failed energy efforts have deprived taxpayers of hundreds of millions of dollars. So why should American families really finance such a distant program?

RECOVERY

To prevent wasteful, unnecessary spending, Congress should include in future appropriations legislation restrictions on the types of grants federal agencies can fund so the grant-funded initiatives clearly advance American national interests.

For more information, please visit:
U.S. Department of State: Morocco: Opportunites for Public Comment
Judicial Watch: U.S. Spends $250,000 to Make Morocco "Green"

TO ADVERTISE OR NOT TO ADVERTISE? THAT IS THE QUESTION.

QUICK STATS

- ✘ **CONFERENCE:** Regulation
- ✘ **TEAM:** Federal Communications Commission
- ○ **FUMBLE:** Not treating all public television stations the same
- ○ **HOW TO RECOVER THE BALL:** FCC should provide equal treatment to all stations

Since the 1930s FCC has reserved some public television channels and radio stations as non-commercial. This practice is intended to allow certain channels and stations to be educational or otherwise beneficial to the public. However, not all channels are treated equally.

Non-Commercial Educational (NCE) Public Interest Obligation (PIO) channels, like KWHB-TV 47 in Tulsa, OK, are not treated the same as Public Broadcasting Stations (PBS). PBS is able to air sponsorships of for-profit entities, which basically function as ads. Those opportunities are not extended to PIOs. Public broadcasting stations can air "sponsorships" from companies but not commercials. Allowing PBS to air commercials would allow growth and would save taxpayers millions in subsidies. Television has changed since the 1930s; it is time Congress catches up.

RECOVERY

FCC should work with all broadcasters to provide equal treatment to all stations to ensure standards are applied uniformly.

For more information, please visit:
The Library of Congress: Committee Reports: Financial Services and General Government Appropriations Bill, 2016
FCC: Nonprofit Media

SOLAR BEER

QUICK STATS

- ✘ **CONFERENCE:** Spending
- ✘ **TEAM:** Department of Agriculture
- ○ **FUMBLE:** $35,000
- ○ **HOW TO RECOVER THE BALL:** Rural Energy Program grants should assist agriculture-related projects, not breweries

Throughout this football season, many tailgaters enjoyed the sun and perhaps an adult beverage. Last year, USDA took the association of sun and suds to an entirely new level. In 2014, USDA awarded a $35,000 grant to install solar panels at a brewery in northern Michigan, which will support seven percent of their annual energy needs.[188] In 2015 a $13,810 grant was awarded to a Wyoming brewery, also to install a solar panel.[189]

The grant for "solar-powered beer" is made possible through the Rural Energy for America Program (REAP), which was created by the Farm Bill in 2002 to help expand renewable energy for farmers and businesses. The program was initiated with laudable intent, but it is doubtful taxpayer support for breweries is within anyone's idea of the proper role of the federal government. This is especially true when the nation has an almost $19 trillion national debt, and families across the country have tightened their belts during tough times.

In an explosion of craft brewery facilities over the last decade, the industry has grown from 1,500 breweries in 2006 to more than 4,000 breweries this year.[190] In 2014 approximately two new breweries opened every day.[191] With a nearly $20 billion market, the resurgence of the craft beer industry is a true American success story.[192] However, continued investment and financial success should be driven by customers not American tax dollars.

RECOVERY

While federally supported beer production may sound reasonable to a few, it is simply not in the national interest. Congress needs to work with the USDA to ensure it remains focused on agriculture.

For more information, please visit:
Taxpayers for Common Sense: Rural Energy for America Program Fact Sheet
USDA: USDA Invests $6.7 Million in 544 Renewable Energy and Energy Efficiency Projects Nationwide

REGULATORY OVERTIME

QUICK STATS

- ✗ **CONFERENCE:** Regulation
- ✗ **TEAM:** Department of Labor
- ○ **FUMBLE:** $1.3 billion per year in lost productivity
- ○ **HOW TO RECOVER THE BALL:** No funds should be issued to implement the regulation

On July 6, 2015, DOL issued a Notice of Proposed Rulemaking on a proposed rule to double the salary threshold exemption for executive, administrative, and professional employees, known as the "EAP" or "white collar" exemption. In other words DOL plans to expand who is eligible for overtime pay for working more than 40 hours a week.[193] This sounds great in a press release, but what is the real effect?

"Worker morale would likely decline," notes the National Federation of Independent Businesses.[194] If a business cannot afford the more expensive overtime pay, it may have to move its low- to mid-level managers, who may make less than the $50,440 threshold, from a salaried position with flexibility and health insurance to an hourly position, which would effectively give give them a demotion.[195] The proposed regulation also completely ignores the cost of living in different areas of the country. In Oklahoma it only takes around $785 to have the same buying power as $970 per week nationally.[196] So DOL drives up payroll costs and hinders small, family-owned businesses' ability to hire more workers.

While DOL wants to forces every company to give people a raise, the clear consequence of the rule will be fewer jobs with benefits in rural America and fewer opportunities to grow into management. The U.S. needs more job opportunities not fewer.

What is the cost for all of this? According to DOL, "[A]s the cost of labor rises due to the requirement to pay the overtime premium, the demand for overtime hours decreases, which results in fewer hours of overtime worked."[197] The proposed rule's analysis estimates the proposal will cost roughly $255 million in direct expenses to employers each year. The annual paperwork burden of the regulation is estimated to be 231,250 hours.[198] The regulation overall will result in 21.2 million hours of lost labor each year, which amounts to $1.3 billion in lost productivity.[199]

RECOVERY

While the rule is not yet finalized, in upcoming appropriations bill Congress could still act to withhold funds for implementation, which would have the effect of preventing the enforcement of the rule. Revoking funds will protect employees and employers from the adverse effects of the proposal.

For more information, please see:
American Action Forum: "White Collar" Overtime Expansion
American Action Forum: Overtime Pay Expansion: Who Will the DOL's New Rule Impact?
DOL: Defining and Delimiting the Exemptions for Executive, Administrative, Professional, Outside Sales and Computer Employees

ESSENTIAL AIR SERVICE

QUICK STATS

- ✗ **CONFERENCE:** Spending
- ✗ **TEAM:** Department of Transportation
- ○ **FUMBLE:** $263 million to fund the Essential Air Service
- ○ **HOW TO RECOVER THE BALL:** Eliminate the program

Flying around the country on personal jet is typically a luxury reserved for the rich and famous. However, travelers to destinations funded by the Essential Air Service (EAS) may find themselves flying solo on a commercial jet sometime soon. The Airline Deregulation Act of 1978 created the EAS program to subsidize commercial flights to small community airports that operated before the deregulation of the airline industry.[200] EAS was intended to be a temporary program to assist these airports with the transition into the free-market system.

However, as Milton Friedman said, "nothing is so permanent as a temporary government program." With expiration looming in 1988, Congress provided the communities another 10 years to wean off the subsidies, eventually backtracking on transition and permanently enacting the EAS in 1996. DOT spent $263 million in FY 2015 to support the traveling convenience subsidies, more than quintuple what it was in 1996 in inflation adjusted dollars.[201]

A CBS investigative analysis found that 44 of the 113 EAS supported flight routes are two-thirds or more empty.[202] This includes a flight a reporter took with only 4 other passengers to Devils Lake, ND, a town of 7,000.[203] This twice-a-day route costs taxpayers $3.2 million annually. Taxpayers also subsidize flights to Hagerstown, MD to the tune of $560 per passenger, even though Dulles International Airport is a short 78-mile drive away.[204] Approximately $1.4 million is spent every year on passengers flying in and out of Franklin/Oil City, PA at a subsidy rate of $927 per passenger, even though Pittsburgh is only 85 miles away. A flight from Kansas City, MO, to Great Bend, KS, serves on average only one passenger per day at the cost of $1.4 million annually, which is subsidized by taxpayers at a cost of $2,626 per person.[205]

Despite some small reforms to restrict program eligibility, spending on EAS continues to steadily rise in order to subsidize flights that often have fewer than ten passengers per day and cost more than $500 per passenger. GAO found that low-cost flights at non-subsidized airports are often more convenient and cheaper than EAS flights.[206] CBO recommended that Congress consider eliminating EAS in its budget options.[207] Congress has yet to act on the recommendation.

RECOVERY

It is simply unfair to expect families in 99 percent of cities to subsidize convenient travel options for passengers flying in and out of the seldom-used 144 EAS airports. Congress should recognize that this 37-year temporary program is no longer essential and should eliminate it.

For more information, please visit:
CRS Report: Essential Air Service
CBS News: Is Essential Air Service wasting taxpayer money?
DOT: EAS Communities
KCTV 5 News: Investigation finds taxpayers fund nearly empty flights
GAO: Commercial Aviation: Status of Air Service to Small Communities and the Federal Programs Involved
CBO: Eliminate the Essential Air Service Program

FEDERAL PROTECTIVE SERVICE FLEET

QUICK STATS

- ✗ **CONFERENCE:** Spending
- ✗ **TEAM:** Federal Protective Service
- ○ **FUMBLE:** $2.5 million mismanagement of vehicle fleet
- ○ **HOW TO RECOVER THE BALL:** Institute greater oversight and cost reductions for the federal vehicle fleet

One federal law enforcement agency has a more generous vehicle give-away program than Oprah. A recent oversight report found that FPS has 101 more law enforcement vehicles than law enforcement positions at an additional cost of $9,500 per year.[208]

FPS, which is under DHS, is tasked with providing security and law enforcement services to more than 9,500 federal facilities across the United States. To accomplish its mission, FPS commands a fleet of more than 1,000 vehicles, which costs American taxpayers more than $10 million annually.[209]

A recent report by the IG for DHS found FPS failed to provide proper oversight and justification for its vehicle fleet size. In addition to the aforementioned excess vehicles, the report found that FPS did not have adequate justification for 32 administrative vehicles, that FPS overwhelmingly used more expensive SUVs without justification for the $1.1 million in additional costs, and that it could not justify 1.2 million miles of home-to-work miles as essential to the agency's mission. In total, FPS's overly generous vehicle fleet policies have cost taxpayers an extra $2.5 million.[210]

Interal agency oversight is vital to ensure employees efficiently utilize resources to accomplish each organization's mission.[211] The FPS report is emblematic of a larger problem within the entire federal government, namely the inability to effectively manage its $4 billion vehicle fleet budget.[212]

According to a 2012 study by GAO, the number of federal vehicles, excluding postal and non-tactical military, increased about seven percent since FY 2005 (from 420,000 to 449,000 vehicles)[213] While these numbers have since decreased, there remain some very questionable vehicle holdings in the fleet, including: 54 SUVs and 18 heavy trucks for the Broadcasting Board of Governors, 63 vehicles for the National Archives, and 92 SUVs for FCC.[214]

RECOVERY

Administrative and legislative efforts are necessary to address ballooning vehicle expenditures. One potential solution would be the enactment of S. 427, the Drive Less' Act introduced by Senator Jeanne Shaheen (NH). The bill seeks to reduce the federal fleet by 20 percent and save the taxpayers $5.6 billion over ten years.[215] This is an important area for Congress to pick up the ball. Hard-working American families pay their taxes each year so their government can properly serve them and not buy vehicles by the truck load.

For more information, please visit:
DHS OIG: The FPS Vehicle Fleet is Not Managed Effectively
GAO: Federal Fleets: Overall Increase in Number of Vehicles Masks That Some Agencies Decreased Their Fleets

CROSS-CULTURAL RAISINS

QUICK STATS

✗ **CONFERENCE:** Spending
✗ **TEAM:** Department of Agriculture
○ **FUMBLE:** $200 million annually
○ **HOW TO RECOVER THE BALL:** Eliminate the Market Access Program

The Raisin Administrative Committee's infamous raisin reserve was the subject of much public scrutiny this summer when the Supreme Court ruled their price control system kept prices artificially high and violated the Fifth amendment in *Horne v. USDA*.[216] While the actions of the raisin lobby to take private property "for public use without just compensation" was rightly ruled unconstitutional, the American people may be surprised to know that the raisin lobby has also taken $38 million in federal funds to pay for overseas marketing costs over the past 17 years.[217] Federal policy simultaneously tried to boost demand through marketing support while maintaining artificial, above-market prices to reduce demand.

Every year, the USDA Foreign Agriculture Service's (FAS) Market Access Program (MAP) gives nearly $200 million in American tax money to companies and trade groups to subsidize the advertising, market research, and travel costs of their overseas product promotions. The MAP is one of five FAS programs that provides $2 billion annually to support foreign market access for U.S. products.[218] Annual winners of the federal funds include successful corporations like Blue Diamond, Sunkist, and Welch's.[219]

One annual recipient of MAP funding, the Raisin Administrative Committee, has received more than $38 million since 1998, including $3 million in FY 2015, to promote their products outside the United States. This generous subsidy is provided in spite of the fact that the Raisin Administrative Committee already produces 99.5 percent of all American raisins and 45 percent of the entire world crop.[220]

Photo: Shutterstock

The Raisin Administrative Committee is a group of 46 California raisin growers and packers who manage the now defunct National Raisin Reserve. As the Supreme Court describes in the origin of the Reserve, "the Agricultural Marketing Agreement Act of 1937 authorizes the Secretary of Agriculture to promulgate 'marketing orders' to help maintain stable markets for particular agricultural products. The marketing order for raisins requires growers in certain years to give a percentage of their crop to the Government, free of charge."[221] This federally ordained market-control policy had the impact of artificially boosting raisin prices. In an 8-1 decision, the Supreme Court ruled in *Horne v. USDA* that the National Raisin Reserve was unconstitutional under the Takings Clause.[222]

While federal policy created increased raisin prices that hurt American shoppers, another federal program used taxpayers dollars to bolster sales in international markets. One example of the use of MAP funds was a $3 million advertising campaign in Japan in the 1990s. The campaign featured the animated dancing raisins and used the theme song "I Heard It through the Grapevine." Tragically the song could not be translated into Japanese, and they just ran the ad in English. The result was incomprehensible shriveled dancing figures that disturbed Japanese children, who thought they were potatoes or chunks of chocolate. Moreover, their four-fingered hands made the viewers think of criminal syndicate members whose little fingers are cut off as an initiation rite. For some reason the Raisin Board struggled to sell their product in Japan during this promotional period, and the U.S. wound up spending $2 on promotional costs for every dollar's worth of raisins that made it to the shelves.[223]

RECOVERY

Federal subsidies for advertising costs total more than $38 million. The federal policy of artificially limiting supply to boost prices is contradictory public policy that costs American families more at the grocery store and on their taxes. The federal policy to support artificially elevated raisin prices was eliminated by the Supreme Court. It is now time for Congress to take the next step and remove federal support for private marketing endeavors for select industries and companies by ending the MAP.

For more information, please visit:
The Wall Street Journal: Supreme Court Strikes Down New Deal-Era Raisin Price-Support Program
USDA: Market Access Program
USDA: Market Development Programs
USDA: MAP Funding Allocations – FY 2015
Fresno County Farm Bureau: What's Being Harvested Now?
Supreme Court of the United States: Opinion: Horne v. Department of Agriculture
IDFA: Testimony Before the Senate Committee on Homeland Security and Governmental Affairs Subcommittee on Federal Spending Oversight and Emergency Management

INDIAN COAL COUNTRY

QUICK STATS

- ✗ **CONFERENCE:** Spending
- ✗ **TEAM:** Internal Revenue Service
- ○ **FUMBLE:** $76 million for a two-year extension of a coal production tax credit
- ○ **HOW TO RECOVER THE BALL:** Sunset the production tax credit and eliminate unnecessary regulatory burdens to economic development in Indian coal country

Over the last few years, conversations involving coal have generally revolved around the federal government's forced retirement of coal-fired power plants. Individuals interested in coal production may find it difficult to believe that some coal subsidies still exist. Since 2005 coal produced in Indian country (areas within the borders or reservation of an Indian Tribe) has been subsidized at about $2 per ton of coal sold.[224] Each time the credit is extended an additional two years, it costs a projected $76 million.[225] The purpose of the subsidy was to make production on Indian lands competitive with coal produced elsewhere and to support historically depressed economies. This is a familiar theme in government; if federal policies and regulations make a product more expensive, Congress simply provides additional financial support for its production. Instead of just writing a check on the taxpayer dime, the federal government needs to look at the reasons why production on Tribal lands is so expensive.

In the two highest coal-producing states, Wyoming and West Virginia, state regulators have primacy over mining programs.[226] However, on Indian lands, the federal government is the regulator, which in turn results in additional permitting requirements that do not exist on state and private lands. These requirements translate to more time and more money spent to develop projects that provide high-paying jobs. BIA and federal regulations have made it so difficult and so expensive to develop energy on Indian land that the government gives a subsidy to incentivize production.

RECOVERY

Finding sustainable ways to grow the economy is critical for the next generation, especially in Indian Country in light of its historically high unemployment rate. Congress should work with Tribes to either allow them to develop their own regulatory process or at least ensure federal regulations enforced in Indian Country are no more stringent than in surrounding areas. This will allow increased energy production and more employment in Tribal areas and also save some of the tax money paid by hard-working American families.

For more information, please visit:
GPO: Committee on the Budget Committee Print
OSMRE: Regulating Coal Mines

$5,000 FIDDLE FILM

QUICK STATS

- ✘ **CONFERENCE:** Spending
- ✘ **TEAM:** National Park Service
- ○ **FUMBLE:** $5,000 documentary on Master Fiddler Roger Howell
- ○ **HOW TO RECOVER THE BALL:** Increase oversight of the grant process

Photo: Roger Howell Documentary Project

Unnecessary federal spending comes in all shapes and sizes, but it all contributes to the massive national debt. This year the Liston B. Ramsey Center for Regional Studies at Mars Hill University in North Carolina was awarded a $5,000 grant to produce a documentary film about Madison County Master Fiddler Roger Howell.[227]

The grant was funded through the Blue Ridge National Heritage Area, part of the NPS National Heritage Partnership Programs. In 2003 Congress designated the Blue Ridge National Heritage area in recognition "of the unique character, culture, and natural beauty of the Blue Ridge Mountains and foothills in Western North Carolina." This legislation also formed a non-profit to oversee the federal funding, develop partnerships in the region, fundraise, and implement projects.[228]

RECOVERY

A $5,000 grant, which is $500 greater than the monthly income of the average American family, does not compare to the billions of dollars of frivolous spending by the federal government each year.[229] However, it is not the federal government's job to increase local tourism. With all due respect to Mr. Howell and his accomplishments, a documentary about a North Carolina fiddler does not benefit the U.S. national interest or the American public. There are surely interested people in North Carolina or fans of Mr. Howell who could have financed the documentary instead.

For more information, please visit:
Blue Ridge National Heritage Area: Grant Award Announcement
Blue Ridge National Heritage Area: About

DRUG DEALS

QUICK STATS

- ✗ **CONFERENCE**: Spending
- ✗ **TEAM:** Departments of Defense & Veterans Affairs
- ○ **FUMBLE:** $100 million annual drug deal for VA and DOD
- ○ **HOW TO RECOVER THE BALL:** Congress should align the structure, statutory parameters, and regulatory guidance across the VA and DOD prescription-buying programs to increase buying power and reduce costs

Most families and businesses know the value of quantity purchasing power. This is a lesson the DOD and VA should learn. In 2012 DOD and VA separately purchased drugs for 18.5 million beneficiaries at a cost of $11.8 billion.

GAO surveyed 83 common drugs purchased by both departments and found that by purchasing the drug at the lower of either DOD's or VA's price, the taxpayer could have realized a combined savings of $120 million in 2012.[230] GAO also found inconsistencies in prescription drug purchasing across Medicare, Medicare-Part D, and DOD. Of the 78 common drugs sampled, Medicare paid the cheapest price, with Medicare-Part D and DOD overpaying by as much as 69 percent.[231]

Imagine two grocery stores selling milk at $2.00 and $2.70, respectively. Would anyone buy the milk at $2.70? Of course they would not, but that is basically what DOD and VA pay. Americans are savvy shoppers; DOD and VA should be as well.

RECOVERY

Those who wore the cloth of our nation have earned the best treatment, best care, and, if needed, the best medicine possible. But if the DOD and VA both buy the same medication, then they should go together to more cost-effectively buy medicine from the private sector. Congress should work with the DOD and VA to ensure they have the proper process and authorization to jointly purchase the medicine needed by our nation's finest.

For more information, please visit:
GAO: Prescription Drugs: Comparison of DOD and VA Direct Purchase Prices
GAO: Prescription Drugs: Comparison of DOD, Medicaid, and Medicare Part D Reimbursement Prices

25,000+ INELIGIBLE FAMILIES IN PUBLIC HOUSING

QUICK STATS

- **CONFERENCE:** Spending
- **TEAM:** Department of Housing and Urban Development
- **FUMBLE:** $104.4 million in 2015
- **HOW TO RECOVER THE BALL:** HUD should help local housing authorities relocate over-income tenants

The HUD IG issued an alarming report in July 2015, revealing that more than 25,000 families receive subsidized public housing despite exceeding HUD maximum income thresholds. The HUD IG found $104.4 million will go to families not qualified for aid instead of those actually in need.[232]

For example one New York City family living in a public housing apartment had a November 2013 annual household income of $497,911, more than seven times the low-income family threshold of $67,100 in New York City.[233] This means that a family in genuine need of housing assistance in New York City cannot move into an apartment because a family significantly over the income level is occupying it.

HUD strongly objected to the IG's findings, arguing that only local housing authorities have the authority to evict over-income tenants and that "evicting over-income families would work against HUD's efforts to deconcentrate poverty in public housing developments."[234] While noting that HUD has limited power over local public housing authorities, the program still fails to help those most in need to afford housing.

RECOVERY

Public housing is designed to be a temporary place for individuals who need help. When individuals and families remain in taxpayer-funded housing after they get back on their feet, they prevent those in need from receiving help and take advantage of their fellow citizens. HUD should clarify the steps local housing authorities need to take to relocate over-income families. HUD recently walked back its initial objections to the IG's findings, but HUD can still do more to prevent waste and mismanagement. Rep. David Jolly (FL) indicated HUD should provide local authorities with guidance, or Congress should change the 1998 Quality Housing and Work Responsibility Act to help over-income tenants move out of public housing to make the space available for Americans who truly need the benefit.[235] This is a good first step, and Congress should immediately consider it to help solve this problem.

For more information, please visit:
The Washington Post: Congressman threatens to strip HUD of $104 million because of public housing tenants who make too much
HUD OIG: Overincome Families Residing in Public Housing Units
The Hill: HUD audit finds 25,000 ineligible families in public housing

EMERGENCY SPENDING FOR AN EMERGING DEBT CRISIS

QUICK STATS

- ✗ **CONFERENCE:** Spending
- ✗ **TEAM:** Departments of State and Health and Human Services
- ○ **FUMBLE:** $2+ billion for 28 patients
- ○ **HOW TO RECOVER THE BALL:** Return excess emergency spending

In 2014, a massive Ebola epidemic spread across west Africa. It took weeks for the U.S. government to develop a plan, but eventually the Administration allotted $5.4 billion in emergency spending for Ebola containment and treatment. American troops and foreign aid were sent to construct 11 treatment centers in west Africa.

After conducting an in-depth investigation, the *New York Times*, published a blistering article in April 2015 that detailed the failure of America's response to Ebola.[236] Their findings showed that after spending hundreds of millions of taxpayer dollars and deploying thousands of troops to west Africa to combat Ebola, only 28 Ebola patients were treated at the 11 treatment centers built by the United States.[237] That is equivalent to around $72 million per patient. A *Washington Post* investigation in January 2015 reported that some of these treatment centers had not treated a single patient.[238]

Ultimately $1.4 billion in State's emergency funds for Ebola remained unobligated as of August 2015.[239] HHS had a whopping $1.49 billion on top of that as of September 2015.[240] Considering the World Health Organization's most recent Ebola situation report announced a grand total of four people in the world contracted Ebola, where is this money going?[241]

RECOVERY

Rather than aimless and reactionary, American foreign aid needs to be strategic and solutions-oriented. While there is some irony in telling Congress to not move too quickly, the knee-jerk response to every crisis causes overreaction. Since the crisis itself has diminished, the money should be returned to the U.S. Treasury since it is no longer needed for its intended purpose. Ebola emergency funds were all borrowed funds. Americans should always be there to help those in need, but the federal government should not waste money.

For more information, please visit:
The New York Times: Ebola Clinics in Liberia are Seen as Misstep in US Relief Effort
The Washington Post: U.S.-built Ebola treatment centers in Liberia are nearly empty as outbreak fades

A DIFFERENT ONE PERCENT

QUICK STATS

- ✘ **CONFERENCE:** Spending
- ✘ **TEAM:** Agency for International Development
- ○ **FUMBLE:** $335 Million of wasted power
- ○ **HOW TO RECOVER THE BALL:** Before beginning an infrastructure project, agencies should conduct a feasibility study and ensure the project can be used for its intended purpose

Photo: SIGAR

Since 2002 the U.S. government has spent $110 billion in reconstruction projects in Afghanistan, including support for the Afghan National Security Forces; developing roads, hospitals, schools and dams; and cracking down on narcotics and corruption in the country.[242] One of those projects, Tarakhil Power Plant, a diesel-fueled power plant constructed outside of Kabul, Afghanistan, was recently highlighted by SIGAR in a federal audit that deemed the power plant as "severely underutilized" with the intermittent use of the costly facility resulting in damage and premature failure.[243]

From February 2014 to April 2015, the Tarakhil plant produced a mere 0.34 percent (that is 1/3 of one percent) of the total power on the Kabul grid and exported just 8,846 megawatt-hours of power, less than one percent of its production capacity. This output fails to meet the purpose and intent of the power plant. The plant was designed and constructed in 2007 as the primary provider of electricity in Kabul and to operate on a continual basis, all of which was clearly defined in the contractor's requirements to build the plant.[244]

What is worse, the intermittent use of the plant is actually causing damage to the infrastructure itself, which was highlighted in a 2014 USAID IG report as "operating on an intermittent—rather than a continuous—basis has resulted in more frequent starts and stops, which place greater wear and tear on the engines and electrical components… This practice, according to the evaluation, resulted in the premature failure of equipment, which over time will increase operations and maintenance costs and could result in 'catastrophic failure.'"[245] After almost ten years, millions of dollars, and little power generation to show for it, it is only now clear what a colossal waste of taxpayer money it turned into.

RECOVERY

Before building a power plant, the U.S. should first determine if the local government can operate it when the U.S. leaves. As the focus transitions to "electrify Africa," the federal government must learn the lesson of the Tarakhil Power Plant. There should be sensible requirements for construction and development, reasonable expectations for use, and a demonstrated need for the project. Regular oversight should be conducted during and after development to ensure the project remains viable.

For more information, please visit:
SIGAR: Special Inspector General for Afghanistan Reconstruction Letter
USAID: Afghanistan Fact Sheet

GOVERNMENT STUDIES OLD CLICHÉ

QUICK STATS

- ✗ **CONFERENCE:** Spending
- ✗ **TEAM:** National Science Foundation
- ○ **FUMBLE:** $149,000
- ○ **HOW TO RECOVER THE BALL:** Raise the standard for meritorious grant proposals and steer more political science funds toward transformative grants

It is an axiom of American cultural norms that politics is a taboo subject in social settings. While it may be a faux pas to engage in this discussion at the next dinner party, the federal government will utilize taxpayer dollars to delve further into the discomfort that people experience when forced to discuss what some consider to be privately held political views.

Last year, NSF awarded a nearly $150,000 grant for a researcher "to better understand which facets of social interaction about politics are most stress inducing, for which kinds of people, and in which contexts."[246] The ultimate goal is to decrease that stress in order to "energize and enfranchise citizens who are discouraged by our current political system."[247] There is no doubt that civil discourse is critical for a more successful and vibrant democracy. But it is doubtful that connecting stress to political interactions is a topic the agency "tasked with keeping the United States at the leading edge of discovery" should spend scarce federal resources to study.[248]

A recent study found that 86 percent of those polled experienced some amount of stress during the preceding month.[249] Nearly 40 percent of respondents stated that hearing about government and politicians contributed to their stress.[250] One could argue that the most stressful thing about politics is the waste and bloat of government spending, including researching topics such as this.

As millions of American families come together this holiday season to enjoy family, food, and football, many dinner conversations will inevitability steer toward politics. Some family members will enjoy sharing their viewpoints while others will shy away or simply be annoyed by the dialogue. Regardless of where one lies on this spectrum, learning that the federal government will spend nearly triple the median American salary to explore this cliché will give more reason for heartburn than just the turkey and gravy.

RECOVERY

Congress should work with NSF to lay out parameters and expectations for grants. Before awarding grants, NSF should show how the funds will advance American interests and fulfill NSF's mission.

For more information, please visit:
NSF: Understanding the Mechanisms for Disengagement from Contentious Political Interaction
The Washington Post: Politicians are the No. 1 cause of daily stress in our lives

CRIME VICTIMS SHOULD NOT BE PAWNS IN BUDGET GAME

QUICK STATS

- ✗ **CONFERENCE:** Spending
- ✗ **TEAM:** Congress
- ○ **FUMBLE:** Using funding for crime victims as a budget gimmick
- ○ **HOW TO RECOVER THE BALL:** Do not take money out of the CVF to pay for other areas of the federal budget

Congress created the Crime Victim Fund (CVF) in 1984 to receive deposits from criminal fines to fund grants to victims' service groups such as child advocacy centers, domestic violence shelters, and rape crisis centers. The CVF was based on the idea that the money collected from people who commit crimes should be used to assist victims.[251]

Instead of supporting crime victims, the CVF has been used to support out-of-control congressional spending habits through an obscure budgetary trick called changes in mandatory spending, or "CHIMPS." In an accounting gimmick that would make Enron proud, CVF CHIMPS allow for Congress to spend the *exact* same money more than ten times over.

It works like this. In 2000 Congress set a cap on funds that can be spent from CVF in a single year.[252] Any funds that have been deposited in CVF above that spending cap must remain in CVF to be used in future fiscal years. Since 2000 the receipts coming into CVF have outpaced spending that is subject to the annual cap. Thus, the CVF account has grown to more than $13 billion.[253]

The catch is, due to poorly conceived budget scorekeeping methods, the difference between the cap on spending from the CVF in a year and the total funds remaining in the CVF is considered "savings" that can be used to offset spending elsewhere. The theory is that if Congress spends $2 billion from a fund that has $13 billion available, then the federal government has saved $11 billion. In reality *not* spending the same $11 billion year after year does not save money at all. As Senator Jeff Sessions (AL) appropriately described this process, "It would be like a family delaying a single $500 home repair for ten years and counting it as $5,000 in savings—$500 for every year the repair didn't take place."[254]

Yet, with this fuzzy congressional math, Congress uses the same $11 billion to justify more than $100 billion in new spending over 10 years.

RECOVERY

Congress should stop trying to trick the American people through dishonest budgetary practices. The CVF should be used to support victims of crime without being raided annually to cover spending somewhere else.

For more information, please visit:
Office for Victims of Crime: About OVC

FED STUDY ON THE UPS AND DOWNS OF SENIOR DATING

QUICK STATS

- ✘ **CONFERENCE:** Spending
- ✘ **TEAM:** National Science Foundation
- ○ **FUMBLE:** $374,087 senior adult dating study
- ○ **HOW TO RECOVER THE BALL:** Require a thorough disclosure and transparency process for federal grants to ensure funding focuses on items of national interest

Photo: Shutterstock

NSF strikes again—this time by funding research intended to delve into the dating habits of single adults over the age of 60. The study, "Understanding Age-Related Changes in Relationship Maintenance Strategies," questions whether the mature population's accumulation of life experience impacts approaches toward conflict in relationships. Apparently the existing "close relationships research," which predominantly centers around the actions of senior adults, will cost taxpayers nearly $375,000.[255]

The study began in the summer of 2015, and completion is estimated for late spring of 2018. That is three years of playing date-doctor with the unclear objective of obtaining a "more comprehensive understanding of relationship maintenance efforts."[256]

RECOVERY

NSF needs to state with greater clarity how research findings can practically benefit policy development. Given the federal government's debilitating debt debacle, Congress needs to determine the spending items that realistically fall within the national interest. Unless this "federal Match.com" for seniors develops policy solutions to bring down the debt, maybe this one is better left to the private sector.

For more information, please visit:
NSF: Understanding Age-Related Changes in Relationship Maintenance Strategies
The Washington Free Beacon: Feds Spend $185,850 Studying the 'Ups and Downs' of Old People's Dating Lives

OUT OF SIGHT, OUT OF DATE, OUT OF LUCK

QUICK STATS

- ✗ **CONFERENCE:** Regulation
- ✗ **TEAM:** All agencies
- ◯ **FUMBLE:** Outdated guidance documents from federal agencies
- ◯ **HOW TO RECOVER THE BALL:** Conduct regular guidance spring cleanings

Federal regulators often use guidance documents to explain and clarify their regulations to the public. Guidance documents cannot impose new legally binding obligations on businesses and individuals—only regulations issued through the formal rulemaking process can do that. However, guidance documents often have the effect of changing the behavior of businesses that seek to avoid unnecessary and costly federal intrusion.

In 2015 GAO found that 11 of the 25 sub-agencies it reviewed did not regularly evaluate whether issued guidance was effective and accurate. In one example DOL's Office of Federal Contract Compliance Programs conducted a two-year review of its existing guidance directives. After reviewing guidance documents in 2012 and 2013, officials discovered more than 85 percent of the office's guidance documents were unnecessary or outdated.[257] While this effort is commendable, it begs the question: how many other agencies have outdated or conflicting guidance on their websites?

Photo: Shutterstock

RECOVERY

Federal agencies must do a better job to ensure their guidance documents are up-to-date and easy to find and meet the needs of regulated parties. On November 17, 2015, the Senate passed two joint resolutions of disapproval with bipartisan support that would prevent the EPA from enforcing the CPP.[258] By conducting guidance spring cleanings like the Office of Federal Contract Compliance Programs, federal agencies can avoid confusion and make it easier for small businesses and other affected entities to comply with federal mandates.[259]

For more information, please visit:
GAO: Regulatory Guidance: Selected Departments Could Strengthen Internal Control and Dissemination Practices
DOL: OFCCP Guidance Documents

EPA'S $8.4 BILLION "CLEAN" POWER PLAN

QUICK STATS

- **CONFERENCE:** Regulation
- **TEAM:** Environmental Protection Agency
- **FUMBLE:** $8.4 billion regulation to re-engineer the U.S. energy policy
- **HOW TO RECOVER THE BALL:** Revoke this rule and develop all-of-the-above energy policies to support American jobs

With an astonishing $8.4 billion price tag, EPA'S new Clean Power Plan (CPP) will drastically raise energy prices for American families and will place undue burdens on the economy.[260] The CPP will force many states to shut down critical power plants without immediate replacement sources of energy for homes and businesses. This means higher costs for families to heat and cool their homes and higher electricity bills for everyone. The CPP claims it gives states the flexibility to meet the 32 percent carbon emissions reduction target. However, in reality many states simply cannot reduce their emissions by 1/3 without abruptly closing existing power plants.[261] In Texas Bloomberg Business reports family electricity bills will jump by as much as 16 percent by 2030, and the CPP will significantly increase the chance of blackouts.[262]

To make matters worse, CPP's devastating impact on the economy is not the rule's only major flaw. Preeminent constitutional scholar (and President Obama's former law professor) Laurence H. Tribe described the CPP as "unconstitutional" in a 2014 *Wall Street Journal* op-ed. Mr. Tribe argues the Clean Air Act forbids EPA from regulating power plants for additional hazardous pollutants that are already regulated by EPA. He goes on to say that what the President could not achieve through the legislative process, he directed EPA to regulate "as though it has the legislative authority... to re-engineer the nation's electric generating system and power grid. It does not."[263] EPA continues to make huge promises of future benefits, but the CPP will certainly increase the cost of every product that uses energy to produce.

RECOVERY

EPA should develop a true, all-of-the-above energy plan that focuses on job growth, affordability, reliability, and sustainability. The Administration is obsessed with killing all forms of carbon-based energy, but it fails to state what is next. Americans use electricity and energy for their homes, businesses, and transportation. Increasing the cost only hurts seniors and those on fixed incomes. Wealthy environmentalists can afford higher prices; most Americans cannot.

For more information, please visit:
EPA: Clean Power Plan for Existing Power Plants
Bloomberg Business: Clean Power Plan to Shutter 4,000 MW of Texas Coal Output
The Wall Street Journal: The Clean Power Plan is Unconstitutional
Science Direct: Employment Trends in the U.S. Electricity Sector

AMBASSADORS (SLUSH) FUND

QUICK STATS

- ✗ **CONFERENCE:** Spending
- ✗ **TEAM:** Department of State
- ◯ **FUMBLE:** $5.75 million
- ◯ **RECOVERY:** U.S. spending abroad should advance American national interests

In 2014, State spent $700,000 to conserve a Buddhist temple in Vietnam[264], $40,000 to document Bengal folk music in India[265], and $33,000 to preserve Jamdani weaving traditions in Bangladesh.[266] Through the years American taxpayer dollars have their been used to pick up the tab to rebuild ancient mud forts in Pakistan,[267] fund a log house museum in Russia,[268] and preserve ancient dialects in South America.[269] The American public has borrowed money from China to fund the construction of a welcome grotto on a Buddhist temple in China.[270]

Projects like these add up to $5.75 million per year in State's annual allocations to its Ambassadors Fund for Cultural Preservation,[271] which is used to support "the preservation of cultural sites, cultural objects, and forms of traditional cultural expression" around the world.[272] While altruistic in nature, there is little room for such feel-good spending on programs that do little to advance Americans interests. There are plenty of avenues for American ambassadors and diplomats to responsibly help other nations, rather than funneling money into international historic reconstruction projects.

RECOVERY

It is not justifiable to expect American families to spend millions to help preserve other nations' cultures—many of whom are capable of preserving their own cultural sites and artifacts. It is past time to end this program once and for all. During the next appropriations season, Congress should simply eliminate the Ambassadors Fund for Cultural Preservation. When Americans complain about foreign aid, this is what they mean.

Photo: State Department

For more information, please visit:
U.S. Department of State: U.S. Ambassadors Fund for Cultural Preservation 2014

AMTRAK'S BOTTOMLESS PIT

QUICK STATS

- ✗ **CONFERENCE:** Spending
- ✗ **TEAM:** Amtrak
- ○ **FUMBLE:** Millions of dollars to subsidize Amtrak's food and beverage service
- ○ **HOW TO RECOVER THE BALL:** Assess the source of financial losses and revise the food and beverage service model to meet the needs of Amtrak's customers

Photo: Twitter

Amtrak has an expensive appetite. Its food and beverage services operate at major losses each year, requiring taxpayers to pick up the difference. From 2006 through 2012, Amtrak suffered $609 million in direct losses from these services alone.[273] While Amtrak lost $105.2 million in 2006 on these services, by 2012 losses were down to only $72 million.

While the trend is headed in the right direction, the Amtrak IG identified some areas Amtrak has yet to truly address. For example 99 percent of revenue losses can be attributed to long-distance routes.[274] Despite knowing this and despite a requirement that food and beverage service not be provided at a loss,[275] the company has yet to adjust the service level on these routes to meet rider demands. Amtrak also continues to staff at regular levels during seasons when ridership is traditionally low. Moreover, food and beverage staff are required to report to work one to five hours before departure time despite staff not needing that amount of time to perform required duties prior to leaving. All of this suggests that Amtrak does not fully understand its staffing needs, which leads to taxpayers unnecessarily picking up the tab for riders' meals.

RECOVERY

This train will continue down a track plagued by fiscal woes as long as subsidies prevent accountability for losses. In government reducing losses from $105.2 million to $72 million is unfortunately a step in the right direction. In business it is a step toward bankruptcy. Congress should work with Amtrak to require it to operate like a business. Business owners around the nation know that if they lose enough money, they will go out of business. Amtrak has unfortunately relied on federal funding so long that it has not moved quickly enough to correct its operations. Americans do not subsidize the food served on planes and should not subsidize the food on trains.

For more information, please visit:
Amtrak OIG: Food and Beverage Service: Potential Opportunities to Reduce Losses
CRS Report: Issues in the Reauthorization of Amtrak

TAXPAYER-FUNDED PROPAGANDA MACHINES

QUICK STATS

- ✘ **CONFERENCE:** Spending
- ✘ **TEAM:** Department of State
- ⭕ **FUMBLE:** $5 million Twitter account
- ⭕ **HOW TO RECOVER THE BALL:** Require metrics for CSCC initiatives

Photo: Screen shot of Twitter

State's Center for Strategic Counterterrorism Communications (CSCC), created under an executive order with a roughly $5 million annual budget,[276] has a fancy name with a 21st century task all middleschoolers can accomplish: it operates a Twitter account. Granted, most seventh graders do not focus their Twitter feeds on telling the "truth about terrorism," but even they would probably agree the oddly titled "Think Again, Turn Away" project tweets to dissuade would-be terrorists from joining the jihadi movement.

Is a $5 million taxpayer-subsidized Twitter account with no way to measure success a good investment for U.S. taxpayers? It is reasonable for American taxpayers, who fund this expensive social media project, to expect there to be metrics on what the mission is, how to define success, and who the target audience is. It is not unreasonable for State to tweet the facts about global terrorism or to work to get the truth out about the murderous thugs of ISIL. There are millions of reasons to "turn away" from terrorism, but should it really cost millions of dollars to tweet about them?

RECOVERY

Congress should require better metrics, or simply metrics at all, for CSCC's initiatives. This project could be beneficial, but it is up to CSCC to prove it. Tax dollars from hard-working American families should be doled out with a reasonable expectation for how the funds will be used. American families put thought and planning into how they spend money. Congress should ensure federal agencies and departments do the same.

For more information, please visit:
Twitter: @ThinkAgain_DOS
The White House: Executive Order 13584 – Developing an Integrated Strategic Counterterrorism Communications Initiative
U.S. Department of State: Center for Strategic Counterterrorism Communications
The Washington Post: In a propaganda war against ISIS, the U.S. tried to play by the enemy's rules

"I SEE DEAD PEOPLE."

QUICK STATS

- X **CONFERENCE:** Spending
- X **TEAM:** Social Security Administration
- O **FUMBLE:** Failure to maintain accurate death records means billions in fraud
- O **HOW TO RECOVER THE BALL:** Pass legislation that requires agencies to ensure all number-holder data is accurate and regularly updated

In what would be a boon for the birthday candle industry, an analysis of SSA files showed that approximately 6.5 million people who are 112 years old or older are still alive.[277] In reality fewer than 40 individuals in the world ever reach that age.

A February 2015 report from SSA's IG found SSA does "not have controls in place to annotate death information on the Numerical Identification System (Numident) records of number holders who exceeded maximum reasonable life expectancies and were likely deceased."[278]

SSA maintains a list of the deceased. Known as the Death Master File (DMF), the list is used as a reference source for many public and private institutions to access accurate data of the American population. SSA gathers death data from funeral homes, state agencies, surviving families, and federal agencies. The IG report found SSA recorded death dates for nearly 1.4 million number-holders in payment records but neglected to transfer this information to the master database.[279] Because other agencies rely on the DMF to prevent payments to the deceased, any slight oversight creates considerable potential for improper payments. Inaccuracies in death data recordings also leave the door wide open for identity theft and fraud, where an individual could access these numbers to "report wages, open bank accounts, obtain credit cards or claim fraudulent tax refunds."[280]

In a ghost story that could only be concocted in Washington, DC, the SSA IG found bank accounts were opened using active Social Security numbers (SSNs) belonging to individuals born in 1886 and 1893. In 2008 an employer reported wages for an individual who actually died in 1962.[281] Overall, the SSA IG analysis found more than 66,000 people were still reporting wages and roughly 4,000 e-verify checks were run on SSNs that belonged to people born before June 16, 1901. Despite being hard-working people, even Americans slow down after reaching 100 years of age. Interestingly enough, some of these hard-working citizens over 112 even registered to vote.

As of now, the scope of waste and fraud resulting from this shoddy documentation remains to be entirely realized. And the problem remains unresolved due to SSA's insistence that it is not in the business of collecting and distributing death records, despite its long history of doing so. Unfortunately deflecting blame does nothing to change the sizable and troublesome gap in death records and fraud.

RECOVERY

The Stopping Improper Payments to Deceased People Act, introduced by Senator Tom Carper (DE), may provide a good step forward in correcting death data discrepancies. The Act would direct SSA to furnish complete data on deceased individuals to all appropriate federal agencies for program integrity purposes. It would also establish procedures to ensure more accurate collection of death data by the possible integration of state and local data.

Moreover, SSA should be able to flag a newly opened bank account, e-verify request, or other activity for an SSN that belongs to a person 112 years of age or older. While the federal government should not prevent anyone from gaining employment, it seems that more often than not, a 115-year-old SSN will be used by a fraudster rather than its rightful owner.

For more information, please visit:
SSA OIG: Audit Report: Numberholders Age 112 or Older Who Did Not Have a Death Entry on the Numident
PBS Newshour: Report: Social Security numbers active for 6.5 million people aged 112
S.1073 – Stopping Improper Payments to Deceased People Act

END-OF-YEAR BINGE SPENDING

QUICK STATS

- ✗ **CONFERENCE:** Spending
- ✗ **TEAM:** Government-wide
- ○ **FUMBLE:** End-of-year spending binge
- ○ **HOW TO RECOVER THE BALL:** Pass timely appropriations bills and test rollover authority through a pilot program

September does not only mark the start of football season. It also marks the last month of the fiscal year. It is the time of year when federal agency and department officials face the "use it or lose it" dilemma, in which they either spend any remaining money in their budget or return the excess funds to Treasury. Unsurprisingly the data show that "use it" is the favored choice.

Federal agency spending rates are generally higher at the end of the year. Government-wide, between 2003 and 2013, "16.9 percent of obligated contract expenditures occurred during the month of September – more than twice what we would expect if spending were split evenly over 12 months at 8.3 percent per month."[282] The worst offender is State, which spent on average 37.8 percent of its budget in September, more than quadruple what the average spend-out rate should be.

As part of the September shop-till-you-drop spree, State purchased a $1 million granite sculpture for its London Embassy, spent nearly $20,000 for books that were used as Christmas gifts, $1.5 million worth of furniture, $26,315 worth of North Face parkas, and $5 million for custom handcrafted stemware.[283] During congressional testimony, a former State employee recounted how a facility manager needed four flower pots for an African embassy but instead ordered a truck full of pots because he wanted to spend excess money in his facilities budget. The four flower pots were put in their proper place while the rest "were unloaded and placed out of sight behind a building where they were left to slowly crumble in the blazing African sun."[284] Remember, all of this is to avoid returning the funds to the U.S. Treasury, which would save the federal government from spending additional tax dollars collected from hard-working American families.

State is not the only agency with an affinity for binge spending at the end of the year. For example, an IG report on FY 2014 Appalachian Regional Commission grants found that 75 percent of funds were awarded in the last quarter of the fiscal year, including 44 percent in September.[285] A recent report conducted by the DOL IG determined that 44 percent ($212.8 million) of the National Emergency Grants distributed between July 2011 and June 2014 were awarded at the last minute in order to avoid expiration of funds.[286]

The spike in year-end spending cannot be completely attributable to the "use it or lose it" phenomenon. However, the inclination to spend available funds and protect a department's budgetary base is real—and so are the wasteful consequences.

RECOVERY

Spending money to avoid losing it is a huge disservice to American taxpayers. Congress should work with federal agencies and departments to disincentivize this binge spending. The first step is for Congress to adopt a budget in a timely fashion so all agencies and departments can expect funding consistency.

Second, Congress should adopt a trial program for select agencies that would allow carryover of funding so instead of binge spending at the end of the fiscal year, the agency knows it will continue to have that funding through the following year. Finally, Congress should also continue its oversight functions by requiring justifications for extraordinary spending in the final months of each fiscal year.

For more information, please visit:
Mercatus Center: Curbing the Surge in Year-End Federal Government Spending
Washington Examiner: Federal bureaucracies go on end-of-year spending sprees to avoid budget cuts
DOL: ETA Needs to Improve Awarding of Year-End National Emergency Grants

THE HYDROLOGY OF HYDRAULIC FRACTURING

QUICK STATS

- ✗ **CONFERENCE:** Regulatory/Spending
- ✗ **TEAM:** Environmental Protection Agency
- ○ **FUMBLE:** $29.1 million to duplicate existing research on hydraulic fracturing
- ○ **HOW TO RECOVER THE BALL:** Examine existing research prior to undertaking new research to prevent duplication

How much is too much to spend to find out something states already figured out? Apparently the federal government thinks $29.1 million is a bargain. Congress directed EPA to study the effect of the oil and gas extraction technique called hydraulic fracturing on drinking water resources and gave it millions of dollars to do so.[287] The project advanced despite research from states, which did not find a connection between hydraulic fracturing (a 70-year-old technology) and ground-water contamination.[288]

After six years of study, EPA concurred with the findings made by state studies. In fact its report reflected common sense. The report concluded that when done correctly and in line with existing state regulations, hydraulic fracturing is a safe technology that does not endanger water resources by itself.[289]

RECOVERY

Everyone wants access to clean water—especially rig workers and local oil and gas companies since they and their families drink from the same local water supplies as everyone else. But the federal government should not abuse taxpayer resources in an attempt to target industries it does not like. In the future Congress and agencies should look to existing research and only invest new money in areas where legitimate gaps in knowledge exist.

To find more information, please visit:
EPA: Assessment of the Potential Impacts of Hydraulic Fracturing for Oil and Gas on Drinking Water Resources
CRS Report: Hydraulic Fracturing and Safe Drinking Water Act Regulatory Issues

OPPORTUNITY COST: THE *OTHER* COST OF COLLEGE

QUICK STATS

- ✘ **CONFERENCE:** Spending
- ✘ **TEAM:** Internal Revenue Service
- ○ **FUMBLE:** Failing to adequately check tax returns
- ○ **HOW TO RECOVER THE BALL:** Collect college enrollment data in a timely fashion that correlates with tax refunds

The U.S. has a world-renowned higher education system that churns out millions of accomplished graduates every year. Yet with all these college graduates the U.S. is unable to adopt a simple fix to the $5.6 billion in fraud in the federal tax credit targeted at college education.[290] The American Opportunity Tax Credit (AOTC) provides a partially refundable tax credit of up to $2,000 for students enrolled in higher education programs. The credit was first made available in tax year 2009 and was extended through 2017.[291]

The AOTC is reserved for individuals who seek a better future, receive an education, and have greater economic success. Many college students work part- to full-time jobs, juggle academics, and even raise families. IRS has a responsibility to ensure students and families have their returns efficiently processed, while eliminating fraudulent claims.

According to a Treasury Inspector General for Tax Administration (TIGTA) report examining 2012 returns, at least 1.7 million taxpayers who claimed the AOTC provided no supporting documentation that a student had attended an academic institution.[292] Another 361,000 claims involved students who were not eligibly enrolled, and 64,000 individuals improperly received credits for students who were claimed on other taxpayers' returns.[293] In fact 250 prisoners improperly received the AOTC.[294] TIGTA concluded that "more than 3.6 million taxpayers (claiming more than 3.8 million students) received more than $5.6 billion in potentially erroneous education credits ($2.5 billion in refundable credits and $3.1 billion in nonrefundable credits)."[295]

RECOVERY

AOTC fraud is so easy because IRS does not get enrollment data from the universities on time. Congress should work with IRS and universities to move the due-date for forms to IRS earlier. It should not take a degree from a higher education institution to come up with a simple and effective solution. $5.6 billion in fraud is too much, even for government work.

For more information, please visit:
Treasury Inspector General for Tax Administration: Billions of Dollars in Potentially Erroneous Education Credits Continue to Be Claimed for Ineligible Students and Institutions

THE LARGEST AND THE HIGHEST

QUICK STATS

- ✘ **CONFERENCE:** Spending
- ✘ **TEAM:** Internal Revenue Service
- ○ **FUMBLE:** $17.7 billion in improper tax credits
- ○ **HOW TO RECOVER THE BALL:** Clarify existing EITC requirements and update the processing system

The Earned Income Tax Credit (EITC) is the nation's largest anti-poverty cash program. It has also earned the ignoble distinction of having the nation's highest improper payment rate.[296] The EITC is a refundable tax credit program enacted in 1975 as an anti-poverty measure that incentivizes work by providing qualified workers a refundable credit on their income taxes. While the EITC is sound in theory, in practice it has yet to live up to the expectation that it will only serve American families truly in need. With an error rate ranging from 23 to 28 percent, an estimated $17.7 billion was erroneously paid in FY 2015, and $133.9 billion in improper payments were made in the last 10 years.[297]

An audit by GAO on improper payments found much of the waste is preventable. The audit attributed EITC's large error rate to a number of factors including, "complexity of the tax law, structure of the program, confusion among eligible claimants, high turnover of eligible claimants, and unscrupulous return preparers."[298] The law's complex eligibility requirements have led to confusion, especially regarding child relationship and residency rules.[299] A 2006-2008 EITC compliance study found the largest issues involved overpayments from the incorrect claiming of a child ($10.4 billion in overpayments). The most frequent recipient error is the misstatement of income ($5.6 billion in overpayments).[300]

Not surprisingly fraud and tax preparer errors also plague the program. Roughly 2/3 of tax returns that claim the EITC were filed by a tax preparer. In a 2014 study GAO found that of a limited sample of 19 paid tax preparers, 17 of them made mistakes when preparing tax returns that resulted in an incorrect refund amount. As GAO reported, "Nearly all of the returns prepared for our undercover investigations were incorrect to some degrees, and several of the preparers gave us incorrect advice, particularly when it came to reporting non-Form W-2 income (i.e., wage income) and the EITC."[301]

The EITC program helps incentivize employment over welfare and helps provide an important transition for low-income workers into the middle class. However, allowing $1 out of every $4 to be doled out erroneously at a rate of more than $15 billion per year is simply unacceptable.

RECOVERY

Congress should explore options to clarify and simplify the qualifications for claiming a child. Additionally Congress should consider creating a two-track process for tax preparers and returns so certified tax preparers would have their submissions prioritized and processed faster. This would allow more time and scrutiny for returns from non-certified preparers. It would also incentivize continuing taxpayer education to combat EITC overpayments from misinformed tax preparers and concentrate more resources on potential fraudulent filings. Such a two-track system would walk the line between compulsory federal certification and continuing education requirements. Programs that encourage Americans to work should be easily accessible not confusing and wasteful.

For more information, please visit:
Payment Accuracy: High-Error Programs
Payment Accuracy: Earned Income Tax Credit (EITC)
GAO: Improper Payments: Remaining Challenges and Strategies for Governmentwide Reduction Efforts
CRS: The Earned Income Tax Credit (EITC): Administrative and Compliance Challenges
GAO: Paid Tax Return Preparers: In a Limited Study, Preparers Made Significant Errors

THE 30-HOUR WORK-WEEK

QUICK STATS

- **CONFERENCE:** Regulation
- **TEAM:** Internal Revenue Service
- **FUMBLE:** $30 billion in regulatory compliance costs
- **HOW TO RECOVER THE BALL:** Pass the Forty Hours is Full Time Act of 2015

Adding insult to injury in the morass of the President's healthcare law is a provision that requires all businesses with at least 50 full-time employees to provide their full-time workers with health insurance coverage. Under the Administration's definition, an employee who works 30 hours per week is considered full-time, which likely comes as a surprise to many employees who work 40 hours and are not compensated for ten hours of overtime.[302]

This mandate was set to take effect in January 2014. But apparently, an election-year implementation was too burdensome for the Administration. So in mid-2013 the White House delayed it until 2015. Luckily for employers, in February 2014 the Administration delayed enforcement of the mandate once again, giving employers with fewer than 100 employees until January 1, 2016, to comply. To be compliant for 2015, these companies were allowed to only provide coverage for up to 70 percent of their full-time employees.[303]

Employers who fail to offer coverage that satisfies the employer mandate are subject to a penalty of up to $3,000 per worker. According to the National Federation Independent Business, "The mandate makes it extremely expensive to cross the 50-employee threshold. For example, a mid-sized restaurant that goes from 49 to 50 employees will face a $40,000 per year penalty. A business who has more than 50 employees can avoid the penalties by simply letting go of employees until they get under 50 or they can replace one full-timer with two part-timers. Estimating the costs of hiring and expanding will be complex and confusing."[304]

RECOVERY

To prevent the further erosion of jobs in the economy and increase job opportunities for American families, Congress should pass--and the President should sign—S. 30, the Forty Hours Is Full Time Act of 2015. This bill, introduced by Senator Susan Collins (ME) and co-sponsored by a bipartisan group of 41 Senators, would modify the formula for calculating the number of full-time workers employed by an applicable large employer subject to the mandate. The bill would also define a "full-time employee" as an employee who works an average of at least 40 hours per week.

For more information, please visit:
NFIB: Employer Mandate CribSheet
American Action Forum: Primer: Employer Mandate
American Action Forum: How the Affordable Care Act and the Employer Mandate Impacts Employers: An Overview

SOLAR BURN

QUICK STATS

- ✗ **CONFERENCE:** Spending
- ✗ **TEAM:** Department of Energy
- ○ **FUMBLE:** $5 billion in solar subsidies
- ○ **HOW TO RECOVER THE BALL:** Eliminate subsidies that interfere with market choice for winning and losing technologies

Photo: Shutterstock

In 2013 American families gave more than $5 billion to the solar industry through a combination of direct expenditures, tax credits, and federally funded research and development.[305] The investment only added 4,750 megawatts of solar energy to American energy generation in 2013.[306] Or put a different way, the taxpayers paid a little more than $1 million dollars for each megawatt added. This may sound like a high amount of additional generation. But if a megawatt of solar power can power about 164 homes, the federal subsidy breaks down to about $6,418 per home now powered by solar.[307]

Even though the industry benefits from a grab bag of subsidies, it still failed to become even a modest contributor to the American energy mix. As recently as 2014 solar energy only approached one percent of total American electricity generation.[308]

Hopefully solar power will one day be a significant contributor to America's base power, but it still remains a small supplemental energy source. In 1979, President Jimmy Carter called for the creation of a "solar bank" to achieve his goal of 20 percent of American energy coming from solar power by the year 2000.[309] More than three decades later, the federal government still creates incentives and subsidies for solar power. With multiple failed solar companies across the nation, it is important to distinguish when jobs are "created" using federal subsidies and when they are created by market demand and efficiency.

RECOVERY

While it is common for young technologies to receive a federal boost in their early years, many energy sources like solar energy are no longer "new." It is time solar energy stands on its own – or at least provides a better return to consumers and taxpayers. Congress should eliminate this subsidy or enact requirements that set a base level of production to qualify.

For more information, please visit:
SEIA: How many homes can be powered by 1 megawatt of solar energy
U.S. Energy Information Administration: Frequently Asked Questions
U.S. Energy Information Administration: Direct Federal Financial Interventions and Subsidies in Energy in FY 2013

FEMA FLAWS COULD MEAN DISASTER FOR DISASTERS

QUICK STATS:

- ✗ **CONFERENCE:** Spending
- ✗ **TEAM:** Federal Emergency Management Agency
- ○ **FUMBLE:** $247 million+ in underutilized technology system
- ○ **HOW TO RECOVER THE BALL:** Exercise congressional oversight to ensure FEMA fully implements funding and their internal procedures to improve efficiency

Americans are sadly too familiar with weather-related tragedies. In neighborhoods all across the nation, tornadoes, floods, or earthquakes have destroyed homes and priceless belongings. In many cases shortly after humanitarian support arrives, so does FEMA with a check to help cover the cost of the damage. For those in immediate need, it is quite a relief—until several months later when they receive letters requesting the money be returned because FEMA realized those individuals did not qualify for funds in the first place.

Congress's evaluation of FEMA's poor response to Hurricane Katrina led to spending $247 million to create the Logistics Supply Chain Management System, which is intended to help the agency work with other parts of the federal government and non-profit aid organizations after a disaster.[310] Unfortunately, a recent audit of the program found FEMA does not seem to know how to actually utilize the system to coordinate aid after a disaster.[311] Apparently part of the reason FEMA could not properly set up the system is that it has not properly trained its employees, which really discredits the American taxpayers' investment of $247 million.[312]

To FEMA's credit, after major tornadic storms in Oklahoma in 2013, the agency successfully cooperated with numerous faith-based and non-profit groups on the ground to provide important assistance to families in need. Oklahomans are grateful for that assistance, but FEMA can certainly work toward greater efficiency.

RECOVERY

Congress needs to continue to exercise its oversight duties to ensure FEMA fully implements the IG's recommendations: (1) conduct an assessment of the LSCMS program to identify resources necessary to ensure effective management and oversight of the program, and (2) develop an internal process to monitor and ensure accurate LSCMS reporting to OMB. FEMA must implement processes and procedures to improve efficiency to ensure that when families receive aid after a disaster, it does not come back a few months later to demand its return.

For more information, please visit:
DHS OIG: FEMA's Logistics Supply Chain Management System May Not Be Effective During a Catastrophic Disaster
FEMA: LSCMS Logistics Supply Chain Management System

NUCLEAR WASTE

QUICK STATS

- ✗ **CONFERENCE:** Spending
- ✗ **TEAM:** Department of Energy
- ○ **FUMBLE:** Poor contract oversight leading to billions of dollars in cost overruns
- ○ **HOW TO RECOVER THE BALL:** Require the DOE to assess what causes projects to run significantly over time and over budget to prevent future runaway spending

How many warnings of poor project management should be necessary for a federal agency to stop wasting billions of dollars? Apparently, DOE needs more than 25.

DOE contracting management has spent 25 years on GAO's high-risk list, which flags areas of government at risk for runaway spending and unnecessary duplication.[313] Many prime examples of poor oversight come from the National Nuclear Security Administration (NNSA) and show these mistakes are not simply rounding errors on the federal government's budget sheet. NNSA's Mixed Oxide (MOX) Fuel Fabrication Facility project, which would enable the disposal of excess weapons plutonium, was estimated to cost $1 billion in 2002. By 2014 the project ballooned to exceed $7.7 billion, and the timeline for completion was delayed by years.[314]

What is troubling is the agency does not appear to learn from these experiences. GAO recommended that NNSA prevent these types of cost escalations and delays by performing a root-cause analysis for projects exceeding their budget or projected timeline by an agency-specified amount in order to assess whether any systematic causes can be avoided in the future.[315] NNSA disagreed with this recommendation, preferring instead to look at budget and timeline problems on a case-by-case basis. It should come as no surprise that in a joint NNSA-DOD project to extend the life of B61 weapons, NNSA realized last year it would cost $3.6 billion more than expected, and NNSA had not fixed its problem.[316]

RECOVERY

When American families start projects, like remodeling their homes they likely start by ensuring their plans fit within their budget. If part of the project starts to cost too much and goes over budget, the family will likely reconsider the project or stop. Congress should help DOE undertake a similar review of its projects to find why cost estimates and timelines have been so badly forecast. Going forward DOE should also ensure it fully analyzes projects to accurately predict costs and times for completion.

For more information, please visit:
GAO: High-Risk Series: An Update
CRS Report: Mixed-Oxide Fuel Fabrication Plant and Plutonium Disposition: Management and Policy Issues
GAO: Testimony Before the Subcommittee on Strategic Forces, U.S. Senate Committee on Armed Services

ADVISING ADVISORS

QUICK STATS

- ✗ **CONFERENCE:** Regulation
- ✗ **TEAM:** Department of Labor
- ○ **FUMBLE:** $2.4 - $5.7 billion over ten years[317]
- ○ **HOW TO RECOVER THE BALL:** Withdraw the rule; work with Congress to address changes, if needed

Federal regulators now want to advise your advisor. Earlier this year the Department of Labor launched a fiduciary rule that expands their control of retirement advice covered by the Employee Retirement Income Security Act of 1974 by including any advice on Individual Retirement Accounts (IRAs) and annuities by investment advisors or brokers. The goal of the newly expanded rule is to prevent any conflict of interest on the part of those suggesting or marketing a specific retirement investment.[318] This sounds complicated, but it is really simple: you can only get advice from people they approve.

Currently advisors for 401(k) or other employee benefit plans are held to a *fiduciary* standard, meaning they must always put a client's interests and account above their own interests (making money for themselves). However, a person serving as an advisor on an IRA or annuity is held to a *suitability* standard, meaning he or she has to reasonably believe the advice given is in the client's best interest. Under the proposed rule, the suitability standard would be replaced by the tougher fiduciary standard. It sounds good, right?

The problem with this change is that it fails to recognize that IRA and annuity accounts tend to be higher risk and come with higher fees or commissions. Under the new rule, a retirement advisor would likely be forced to only recommend utilizing safer, lower-yield 401(k) or other retirement accounts that also come with lower fees. This is especially true for those investors who have a smaller amount of money to invest. It is very likely that advisors would be afraid to violate their "fiduciary duty" by recommending IRAs or annuities due to the risk that the investments could lose money. At the same time, investors would lose out on advice that could potentially bring much higher returns.[319]

Because the risk is higher for middle-class clients, the new rule also means that most advisors will only take wealthy clients. It will thus be harder for most Americans to get good financial advice except from big investment firms. Ultimately this rule will make the big investment companies bigger and cause the small companies to go out of business.

RECOVERY

Why is the Department of Labor even in the business of regulating financial services when SEC already exists for that purpose? DOL should withdraw this rule, and Congress, in consultation with SEC and financial advisors, should consider whether changes to the current rule are necessary. If changes are needed, Congress should enact legislation instead of allowing a federal agency to create a new rule.

For more information, please visit:
DOL: Fiduciary Investment Advice
Pensions & Investments: DOL moving forward on new fiduciary standard

WATCH OUT FOR SNAILS!

QUICK STATS

- ✘ **CONFERENCE:** Spending
- ✘ **TEAM:** National Science Foundation
- ○ **FUMBLE:** $50,000 snail card game
- ○ **HOW TO RECOVER THE BALL:** Withdraw the rule; work with Congress to address changes, if needed

Federal waste is on the rise, and unfortunately it is not moving at a snail's pace. NSF provided a $50,000 grant to support a project named "Killer Snail: An Interactive Marine Biodiversity Learning Tool."[320] This project is intended to target elementary school students through the development of "an eBook dramatic story told from a snail's point of view, and a mobile video game allowing players to experience and explore the life of marine snails."[321]

Thus far, it appears the grant money has only yielded a physical game. *Killer Snails: Assassins of the Seas* is a card game in which the player has to "collect predatory cone snails that prey on fish, worms and other mollusks, to build a venom arsenal of potentially life-saving peptide toxins. Race your opponents to create the winning venom cocktail and win the game!"[322] While support for technological innovations in education should be driven by state and local funding along with private enterprise, the federal government also supports the use of technology in education through DOEd. For example, DOEd's Small Business Innovation Research program within the Institute of Education Sciences provides more than $1 million annually to "small business firms and partners for the research and development of commercially viable education technology products."[323] Additionally, in October 2014 DOEd and the White House Office of Science and Technology Policy hosted an Ed Games week that culminated with the White House Education Game Jam.[324] The event brought together "more than 100 game developers plus 35 teachers, learning researchers, and students gathered together to develop compelling educational software to help teach complex school subjects."[325]

The Killer Snail project is hardly a compelling use of NSF funds, especially when the national debt continues to climb to almost $19 trillion and other agencies support similar causes. Although creativity is admirable, one has to question the allocation of taxpayer funds to a video game and e-book about a snail, no matter how lethal it may be.

RECOVERY

Congress should work with NSF to ensure it does not fund an area already funded by another part of the federal government. Education activities should be handled by DOEd. The money received from American taxpayers should be utilized in the most efficient way possible, which means federal agencies and departments should avoid duplicative funding.

For more information, please visit:
NSF: I-Corps: Killer Snail: An interactive marine biodiversity learning tool
American Museum of Natural History: Teen Programs: Killer Snails

THE EXCEPTION SHOULD NOT BE THE RULE

QUICK STATS

- **CONFERENCE:** Regulation
- **TEAM:** Departments of Commerce and the Treasury
- **FUMBLE:** Invoking "foreign affairs" exceptions in the rulemaking process to issue rules quickly and without deliberation
- **HOW TO RECOVER THE BALL:** Only use the exception in instances where it is truly necessary

In 1946 Congress enacted the Administrative Procedure Act (APA), which lays out the process for administrative rulemaking. The APA has exemptions for several categories, one of which is foreign affairs. Any rules that involve a "foreign affairs function" are exempt from the rulemaking procedures, which means the Administration does not have to provide any notice and the public is not given an opportunity to comment on the proposed rule. The rule can just be announced and enforced. While the exception is important for matters of national security—especially those that are time sensitive and necessary to quickly protect citizens—it is not intended to be an absolute. It was designed to be used in cases that would "clearly provoke definitely undesirable international consequences."[326]

To meet President Obama's announced policy changes regarding travel and trade with Cuba on December 17, 2014, both Treasury[327] and DOC[328] used the foreign affairs exception to publish new rules on the U.S.'s relationship with Cuba. The U.S. has not had formal diplomatic relations with Cuba since 1961, and as the President noted, Cuba remains a nation governed by the Communist Party. After multiple letters back and forth among the agencies involved, neither could identify a time-sensitive reason to invoke the foreign affairs exception. Given this drastic shift in American foreign policy, the public should have been afforded an opportunity to comment—especially those Cuban-American families who have been impacted by the Castro regime. Providing notice and seeking input from the American people is surely not an undesirable consequence.

RECOVERY

Congress should work with the Administration to tighten the foreign affairs exemption to ensure that necessary leeway remains when making foreign policy decisions and that rules that change decades of U.S. policy are created with public input. The President cannot just create a new policy that allows him to make any change in any regulation as long as he says it is for "foreign affairs."

We are still a nation of the people, by the people, and for the people. If anyone in Washington, DC, cuts out the American people from the process, we have centralized power and silenced the voices of millions of people. There is a right thing to do and a right way to do it.

For more information, please visit:
DOJ: Administrative Procedure Act: Report of the Committee on the Judiciary
DOC: Fact Sheet: U.S. Department Of Commerce and U.S. Department Of The Treasury Announcement Of Regulatory Amendments To The Cuba Sanctions

$40 MILLION TO SUPPORT "ONE OF THE FINEST HOTELS ANYWHERE IN THE WORLD"

QUICK STATS

- ✗ **CONFERENCE**: Spending
- ✗ **TEAM**: Internal Revenue Service
- ○ **FUMBLE**: $40 million
- ○ **HOW TO RECOVER THE BALL**: Eliminate the national historic tax credit

Photo: Shutterstock

Each year many American families will undertake some kind of repair or remodel project around their houses. This may mean repainting a hallway, replacing a sink, or even installing a new roof. It is unlikely that many families will receive federal funding for their home repair projects, even if the home is old. However, companies renovating old and historic buildings might qualify for federal funding or tax credits for the repairs.

In June 2013, the Trump Organization was selected as the developer of the Old Post Office in Washington, DC, in what the organization claims to be "the most sought-after hotel re-development opportunity in the country."[329] The Trump Organization is investing $200 million to renovate the prime real estate into a five-star hotel that will be "in a level of luxury previously unseen in this market."[330] When all is said and done, American taxpayers will chip in $40 million to help cover the costs to "restore this magnificent building to even well beyond its original grandeur."[331]

The taxpayer-funded partnership to subisidize the development of old buildings is made possible by the National Historic Tax Credit. The credit allows an investor to claim 20 percent of rehabilitation costs for certified historic structures (or structures in historic districts) and ten percent of rehabilitation costs for buildings built prior to 1936.[332] The tax credit has repeatedly been used to offset the massive price tags for megaprojects—like Boston's Fenway Park ($40 million) and a resort on Millionaire's Row in Miami, FL ($60 million)—that do not need the help of the American people.[333]

The taxpayer-supported hotel will feature "272 richly furnished guestrooms...with lofty 16-foot ceilings, soaring windows, beautifully restored historic millwork, and glittering crystal sconces and chandeliers."[334] One of the two presidential suites will be 5,000 square feet—twice the average size of an American family home.[335] Each of the suites will include "original fireplaces, wood doors and moldings, and offer unique amenities such as separate dining room with pantry and service entry, his-and-her walk-in closets, private sauna and steam room, two-person shower, and VIP direct-elevator access."[336] Hotel guests will also be able to enjoy a 5,000-square-foot super luxury spa and state-of-the-art fitness center.

While the lucky guests of this palatial hotel will be awestruck by its glitz and glamour, taxpayers are unlikely to be amused that they helped foot the bill through a $40 million tax credit thanks to the National Historic Tax Credit.[337]

RECOVERY

The National Historic Tax Credit is duplicative, untargeted, costly, and distortive. The credit also costs about $1 billion per year in lost revenue.[338] Eliminating the tax break would not prevent states and localities from implementing, maintaining, or expanding their own historic preservation programs. Eliminating the tax credit would also not lead to the collapse of iconic historic structures that have long been protected and preserved by the federal government. Instead its elimination will prevent the federal government from doling out hundreds of millions of dollars to luxury vacation destinations, major league baseball teams, and practically any other renovation project in a building that is included in the not-so-selective list of more than one million buildings on the National Register of Historic Places.

For more information, please visit:
NPS: National Historic Tax Credit
NPS: FY2014 Annual Report on Federal Tax Incentives for Rehabilitating Historic Buildings

TAXPAYERS GET THEIR KICKS ON ROUTE 66

QUICK STATS

- ✘ **CONFERENCE:** Spending
- ✘ **TEAM:** National Park Service
- ○ **FUMBLE:** $287,000 annually to support the Route 66 Preservation Program
- ○ **HOW TO RECOVER THE BALL:** Eliminate the Route 66 Preservation Program

Photo: Shutterstock

According to the American Society of Civil Engineers, Americans spend the equivalent of $101 billion every year on wasted time and fuel on congested major urban highways, in large part due to a lack of capital investment.[339] On roads controlled by the Federal Highway System that cross lands controlled by federal agencies such as the Forest Service, National Parks, and Corps of Engineer properties, the federal government has accrued an $11.55 billion deferred maintenance backlog.[340]

Yet in 2015 a federal grant program provided $20,565 to restore an architectural neon sign at a motel adjacent to Historic Route 66. The grant originated from the Route 66 Preservation Program, an NPS program that provides $287,000[341] annually in grants for the "restoration of restaurants, motels, gas stations and neon signs, as well as for planning, research, and educational initiatives."[342] While this program represents a drop in the bucket compared to the massive shortfalls cited above, it does highlight Congress's inability to learn lessons many parents work to teach their children: the difference between "wants" and "needs."

In 1999 the Route 66 Preservation Program began as a temporary, ten-year grant program to help jumpstart preservation efforts on Route 66. Since 2001, more than 100 grants have been issued for projects along the iconic Route 66 corridor. Federal backing of the program was originally scheduled to terminate in 2009 and transition to a non-federal entity. However, in 2008 the once-temporary program was extended for an additional 10 years, protecting it and its low-priority spending through 2019.

This year's projects include a $25,000 grant for the "Women on the Mother Road: Route 66 Interactive Website and Oral History Project," $20,565 for the Boots Court Roof Restoration in Carthage, MO, and $30,800 for structural restoration to the 1950s Lake Shore Motel, currently known as the Best Budget Inn, in Carthage MO. Grants were also awarded to renovate an abandoned gas station in Oklahoma and a theatre production in Arizona. The program has spent more than $200,000 to restore neon road signs, like the one mentioned above.[343]

Route 66 is an iconic highway that should and will remain an important part in the American story. However, its historical and cultural significance does not depend on taxpayer support for refurbishing roadside attractions.

RECOVERY

Congress should cancel further appropriations for the program and transition the service to a non-federal entity, which was supposed to occur six years ago. Fortunately, there are at least 15 organizations dedicated to Route 66 that are ready to carry the torch of preserving America's Mother Road.[344]

For more information, please visit:
GPO: Route 66 Corridor, U.S. Senate Committee on Energy and Natural Resources Report
NPS: H.R. 146 Omnibus Public Land Management Act of 2009
NPS: Route 66 Corridor Preservation Program

TELL ME HOW MUCH YOU MAKE

QUICK STATS

- ✗ **CONFERENCE:** Regulation
- ✗ **TEAM:** Securities and Exchange Commission
- ◯ **FUMBLE:** $315 Million to enact the "Pay Ratio Disclosure" rule
- ◯ **HOW TO RECOVER THE BALL:** Pass regulatory reform legislation that eliminates unnecessary burdens from the backs of America's businesses

With 141 rules and regulations yet to be finalized as part of the financial regulations imposed by the Dodd-Frank Act, American businesses will have a wealth of opportunies to be subjected to new regulatory burdens and higher compliance costs. Unfortunately, these costs will be passed on to American consumers. Most recently SEC finalized the Pay Ratio Disclosure Rule, which requires all publicly traded companies to report annually the ratio of the average employee's median salary to the salary of the CEO.[345]

After hearing from thousands of businesses and other groups, the federal government estimated the rule's total regulatory compliance cost will be more than $315 million. Compliance will also require 2.3 million hours of company personnel time.[346] However, as American businesses have witnessed too many times, regulatory costs often exceed initial federal estimates—likely because regulators do not adequately communicate with those who will operate under the regulations to allow them to suggest possible consequences of a rule's implementation.

For more information, please visit:
Federal Register: SEC Rule and Cost Estimates
The New York Times: SEC Approves Rules on CEO Pay Ratio
Davis Polk: Dodd-Frank Progress Report

Some in Congress and SEC believe that if companies had to publicly reveal their CEO's salary and the average salary of other employees, it would shame companies into paying CEOs less. In reality the complicated regulation will only make consumers pay more.

Five years after passage, the Dodd-Frank legislation still racks up huge compliance costs to the private sector and requires countless hours in additional personnel paperwork.[347] Of course the cost for all this compliance is passed on to consumers in higher prices.

RECOVERY

The Pay Ratio Disclosure Rule is a good example of the significant regulatory burden Dodd-Frank continually imposes on businesses of all sizes. These costs are then passed on to consumers in the form of higher prices. Congress should move to eliminate these overly burdensome rules, recognizing that it is not the task of the government to shame people.

IDENTITY THEFT TAX FRAUD

QUICK STATS

- ✗ **CONFERENCE:** Spending
- ✗ **TEAM:** Internal Revenue Service
- ○ **FUMBLE:** More than $5 billion in fraudulent refunds
- ○ **HOW TO RECOVER THE BALL:** Implement accelerated W-2s and identity verification processes

Every year IRS issues more than $300 billion in tax refunds to more than 110 million taxpayers. For most taxpayers it is a day when they can get some of their hard-earned money back. For others it is the beginning of a nightmarish realization that someone stole their identities and filed fraudulent returns on their behalf. Billions of dollars in fraudulent returns are paid out every year, and the problem may only get worse. IRS estimates it paid $5.2 billion in fraudulent identity theft refunds in 2013, but that amount could explode to $21 billion as soon as next year.[348]

Fraudsters take advantage of IRS's "pay first, ask questions later" refund model. Under the "look-back" approach, "Rather than holding refunds until completing all compliance checks, IRS issues refunds after conducting selected reviews."[349] Because of the timing, IRS issues refunds months before they can match and verify the information with the W-2s. According to a GAO report on this process, by March 1, 2012, IRS had issued about 50 percent of all 2012 refunds before accessing the W-2 data verified by the SSA.[350] As GAO notes, "If IRS had access to W-2 data earlier—through accelerated W-2 deadlines and increased electronic filing of W-2s—it could conduct pre-refund matching and identify discrepancies to prevent the issuance of billions in fraudulent refunds."[351]

In many ways the IRS tax refund system is similar to the pay-and-chase scheme that has plagued the American healthcare system. The best way to combat identity theft tax fraud is to have a robust pre-refund strategy rather than try to recover funds after they are issued. GAO notes that, "Recapturing a fraudulent refund after it is issued can be challenging—if not impossible—because identity thieves often spend or transfer the funds immediately, making them very difficult to trace."[352]

RECOVERY

If Congress designed the system from scratch today, no one would come up with such a deeply flawed tax process. But since Americans are used to getting their returns at a certain date and time every year, there is reluctance to transition the refund and implement stronger matching and anti-fraud measures. The dollar and social costs of identity theft are too great for the traditional date of returns to remain the same. Congress should consider accelerated W-2s and delayed tax refunds until the W-2s are verified by IRS. This could apply pressure to incentivize employers to submit W-2s earlier. Even though matching W-2s prior to refunds could cause a few refund delays, it will likely only be a one-time transition issue for the taxpayer. Ultimately American taxpayers should be able to trust their government to safely process their most secure information and create efficient practices to combat fraudulent identity claims.

For more information, please visit:
CNBC: Tax-refund fraud to hit $21 billion, and there's little the IRS can do
GAO: Identity Theft: Additional Actions Could Help IRS Combat the Large, Evolving Threat of Refund Fraud
GAO: Report: Identity Theft: Additional Actions Could Help IRS Combat the Large, Evolving Threat of Refund Fraud

ARREST THE OFFICE OF JUVENILE JUSTICE

QUICK STATS

- **CONFERENCE:** Spending
- **TEAM:** Department of Justice, Office of Juvenile Justice and Delinquency Prevention
- **FUMBLE:** An inefficient bureaucratic system where the vast majority of funding for child abuse victims cannot be used during the original 12-month project period
- **HOW TO RECOVER THE BALL:** Create a system to ensure funding can actually be used

The Office of Juvenile Justice and Delinquency Prevention (OJJDP) awarded 28 Victims of Child Abuse Act grants from FY 2010-2013, totaling about $74 million.[353] The grants address important needs for the most vulnerable in American society: children who have been abused. The funding helps develop child-abuse investigations and prosecution programs and funds national organizations to provide assistance to attorneys and others involved in the criminal prosecution of child abuse.[354]

For the 28 grants, on average grantees spent less than 20 percent of the grant during the project's original 12-month period.[355] According to GAO that is due to OJJDP's inefficient administrative review and approval processes that have severely delayed grantees' ability to utilize their funds. This is a waste of both time and resources that could be spent helping an abused child. Abused children, attorneys, and other advocates who step up to help them should not have to waste months wading through processes so they can actually use the funding.

More importantly this is a missed opportunity. Victims of child abuse deserve the absolute best care possible. If the federal government makes the commitment to step up and help a child in need, it absolutely must do it. If the federal government cannot do that, it needs to step back and allow a non-profit or private entity that specializes in this area—such as a church in the child's community—to deliver the essential assistance.

RECOVERY

Congress needs to immediately demand that the OJJDP develop a working system to ensure the most children possible benefit from the available aid.

For more information, please visit:
GAO: Victims of Child Abuse Act: Further Actions Needed to Ensure Timely Use of Grant Funds and Assess Grantee Performance
DOJ: Office of Juvenile Justice and Delinquency Program

LET WASHINGTON, DC, PICK YOUR NEIGHBORHOOD

QUICK STATS

- ✗ **CONFERENCE:** Regulation
- ✗ **TEAM:** Department of Housing and Urban Development
- ○ **FUMBLE:** Federal planning for local communities
- ○ **HOW TO RECOVER THE BALL:** Allow families to decide where to raise their children

People in Washington, DC, already pick Americans' street signs, storm drains, and mortgages, so why not let DC choose people's neighbors? HUD put forth the "Affirmatively Furthering Fair Housing" regulation in August 2015 in order to increase diversity in wealthy American neighborhoods and reduce housing discrimination.[356] The 377-page rule will require communities to develop plans to address segregation and submit their plans to HUD. Specific federal funding will be contingent on the adequacy of a community's plan, which is determined by HUD.

Discrimination in neighborhoods, either in the ownership or rental market, is unacceptable. Under the Fair Housing Act, HUD has authority to address and fight it. HUD should and does use that authority because discrimination based on race, color, national origin, religion, sex, familial status, or disability is illegal.[357] But new regulations that make a federal housing agency the ultimate arbiter of neighborhood design and tie federal funding to specific plans directly contradict what many communities want for the future. With unique and valuable histories, local communities and states understand the needs of their residents better than the federal government.[358] Sweeping federal regulations inhibit flexibility that states say they need to end housing discrimination.

RECOVERY

In addition to forcing misguided federal central planning on American towns and cities, HUD estimates the rule will cost 1,250 local governments a total of $25 million in compliance costs each year.[359] If left unchecked, the regulation will grant the federal government colossal power over states and localities. The Local Zoning and Property Rights Protection Act, introduced by Rep. Paul Gosar (AZ), would repeal the rule and require HUD to consult with state and local public housing officials to develop recommendations to further the Fair Housing Act's original purpose of ending housing discrimination.[360] Families know best where they want to raise their children. This is not a decision the federal government should attempt to make.

For more information, please visit:
Federal Register: Affirmatively Furthering Fair Housing
The Hill: Obama making bid to diversify wealthy neighborhoods
H.R. 1995 – Local Zoning and Property Rights Protection Act of 2015
Rasmussen Reports: Voters Say No to Government Role in Neighborhood Diversity

CO-OP COLLAPSE

QUICK STATS

✘ **CONFERENCE:** Spending
✘ **TEAM:** Department of Health and Human Services
○ **FUMBLE:** $2.4 billion for Obamacare Co-Ops
○ **HOW TO RECOVER THE BALL:** Recover lost dollars; no more funds for failed co-op programs

The President's healthcare law established a billion-dollar, low-interest loan program to create health insurance "co-ops," which were meant to be nonprofit health insurance start-ups to spur competition with insurance companies and drive down costs. More than $2 billion in loans went out, and 23 co-ops opened their doors.[361]

The HHS IG found that by the end of 2014, most of the 23 co-ops "had not met their initial program enrollment and profitability projections."[362] And just like that, co-ops began closing their doors. Co-ops in Iowa, Nebraska, Louisiana, Nevada, and New York shut down. In the week from October 9 to 16 alone, co-ops in four states announced they would close.[363] More than half of the co-ops will have shut their doors by the end of this year.[364] This leaves thousands of patients at risk and the taxpayers on the hook for not only skyrocketing premiums but also billions of wasted dollars on a program that could not achieve its stated goal of low-cost health insurance. For example, in Oklahoma some plans will see a 35-percent premium increase in 2016.[365]

RECOVERY

While little may be done to reclaim the millions of lost dollars, HHS should certainly try. In the meantime Congress has at least not extended any additional loans for the failed co-op program. Congress should fulfill its oversight role by expanding on the IG report to determine how the failure could have been prevented—probably by never creating the insurance co-ops in the first place. Until then at least stop spending more on a failed experiment with partially government-run insurance companies.

For more information, please visit:
Senate Republican Policy Committee: Obamacare into 2016 Showing More Signs of Failure
HHS OIG: Affordable Care Act Enrollment and Profitability Report

TWO IS NOT BETTER THAN ONE

QUICK STATS

- ✘ **CONFERENCE:** Spending
- ✘ **TEAM:** Department of Justice
- ◯ **FUMBLE:** Duplicative bulletproof vest programs
- ◯ **HOW TO RECOVER THE BALL:** Streamline federal programs to reduce overhead and administrative costs to the programs, allowing more federal funds to be used for bulletproof vests instead of bureaucracy

The safety of law enforcement officers who patrol the streets of American communities to protect families is immensely important. One of the best ways the federal government can help them stay safe is to ensure they all have bulletproof vests—a costly but necessary piece of equipment. Unfortunately the best intentions have actually resulted in multiple federal programs to fund and access bulletproof vests for law enforcement officers.

The DOJ's Edward Byrne Memorial Justice Assistance Grant (JAG) Program[366] and the Bulletproof Vest Program (BVP)[367] both provide bulletproof vests to state and local law enforcement through grants to local law enforcement entities. In its FY 2016 budget request, the DOJ requested to designate the BVP as part of the Byrne JAG program instead of BVP representing a separate line-item in the budget with separate costs for overhead and procedures to administer the program.[368] By removing the administrative costs from one program, more money would actually be available to put bulletproof vests on law enforcement officers who need them.

RECOVERY

Congress must find ways to streamline programs and reduce duplication in the federal government. Providing bulletproof vests to American police officers is a good thing, but it does not take two programs to do it. Having two programs that provide the same thing is not fiscally responsible.

For more information, please visit:
CRS Report: FY2016 Appropriations for the Department of Justice
DOJ: 2016 Proposed Appropriations Language

BUY MORE OR FIX WHAT YOU HAVE?

QUICK STATS

- ✗ **CONFERENCE:** Spending
- ✗ **TEAM:** National Park Service
- ○ **FUMBLE:** Mismanaging current assets and spending millions acquiring more
- ○ **HOW TO RECOVER THE BALL:** Addressing current maintenance backlog with LWCF funds

Perhaps the most popular and often-visited federal entity, National Park Service protects and preserves America's greatest landscapes and proudest historical monuments. Unfortunately for the American public, the stewardship of these sites was placed in the hands of Congress, which has neglected to perform the simple duty of tending U.S. national treasures. Instead Congress decided to focus on expanding the federal footprint by spending hundreds of millions of dollars to acquire additional land each year. Meanwhile the federal government has completely lost the ability to care for the lands it already controls. The result of this congressional fumble is about $20 billion in deferred maintenance needs accrued on federal lands, including $11.5 billion in NPS.[369]

Despite federal ownership of 29 percent of all the land in the U.S., Congress spent $1.7 billion over the last ten years (including $178 million in 2015) to acquire additional land through the Land and Water Conservation Fund (LWCF).[370] Unfortunately these purchases do not always come at a cheap price per acre. In the FY 2016 land acquisition priority list, NPS asked to purchase land in Alaska for $400,000 per acre, four acres in Florida for $324,000 ($81,000 per acre), and two acres in Washington for $790,000 per acre.[371]

At the same time these expensive land purchases push forward, failing 70-year-old sewer lines in Yosemite National Park caused raw sewage spills nearly a decade after the deficiencies were reported in a 2006 conditional assessment. The State of California has threatened $5,000 per day in fines if a sewage spill occurs again and $10,000 per day if it reaches the river. NPS warns that "if another major spill occurs, a shutdown of wastewater flows from Yosemite Valley and Yosemite View Lodge facilities will impact visitation by closing facilities served by the trunk main resulting in impacts for visitors and a major loss of revenue to the concessioners, park partners and the park."[372]

Not only is the river in danger, so are some of the most famous trees in America. Deteriorated water pipes first installed in 1932 in the Grove area at Yosemite National Park leak 39,500 gallons of chlorinated water per day. The leaks impact the natural hydrological flow, which damages the health of the 500 mature sequoias that are about 2,000 years old. An expert on sequoias speculated the death of a giant sequoia "may be attributed to the over-abundance of water resulting from the water line leakage."[373]

In New Mexico a failing electrical system caused the loss of power for 21 days, threatens emergency access and could create wildfires at Bandelier National Monument. Even right in Congress's front yard, the water conveyance system on the National Mall is a "dilapidated and complex network of water lines" that was "installed by the War Department of the early 1900s."[374]

NPS's purpose is to preserve and ensure the federal government is a good steward of America's historical monuments and landscapes for generations to come. However, in conjunction with Congress, NPS failed to adequately manage and finance its entrusted assets. If the federal government continues the practice of funding expansion over preservation, the maintenance backlog will continue to grow and the enjoyment of America's most treasured landmarks will be unavailable to future generations.

RECOVERY

Congress must correct its priorities and allow the LWCF to also be used to take care of the deferred maintenance backlog that impacts the access and enjoyment of federal lands and cherished places that the federal government has a duty to protect. American families should not buy cars if they cannot afford gas, and the federal government should not buy more land if it cannot manage the land for the future.

For more information, please visit:
CRS: Land and Water Conservation Fund: Overview, Funding History, and Issues
NPS: Fiscal Year 2016 Budget Justifications
National Parks Traveler: Plans To Restore Mariposa Grove Of Giant Sequoias In Yosemite National Park Open For Comments

PRICEY EMPTY ROOMS

QUICK STATS

- ✗ **CONFERENCE:** Spending
- ✗ **TEAM:** Government-wide
- ◯ **FUMBLE:** $1.67 billion to manage 77,700 unused or under-utilized properties
- ◯ **HOW TO RECOVER THE BALL:** Streamline disposal processes and improve accuracy and accessibility of federal real property database

Photo: Shutterstock

With more than 900,000 buildings and structures totaling a combined area of three billion square feet, the U.S. government has an extensive and varied collection of real estate holdings.[375] While many of the holdings are critical for providing government services, interspersed throughout this collection of viable and necessary properties are approximately 77,700 unused or underutilized federally owned properties.[376] As of 2010 $1.67 billion was spent to maintain these unused or underutilized properties.[377] In other words the federal government spent a large amount of taxpayer money to take care of property that is seldom—if ever—used.

Instead of getting rid of these properties, many of the agencies hold on to them because the "legal and budgetary disincentives" of a sale outweigh the benefits of getting rid of a property.[378] That is government speak for "it is too hard." GAO has consistently noted that selling property is hindered by "statutory disposal requirements, the cost of preparing properties for disposal, conflicts with stakeholders, and a lack of accurate data."[379] Federal real property management has been on GAO's high-risk list since 2003.[380]

The process for disposing of properties is also further complicated by the McKinney-Vento Homeless Assistance Act, which requires agencies to submit a list of excess properties to HUD for a review of whether properties are suitable for use as homeless assistance facilities before they can be sold. A GAO investigation found that many private or non-profit agencies will not use federal properties because they are not practical as homeless assistance centers, but the requirement remains.[381] One glaring example of this problem is that DOI is required to report to HUD on numerous small, remotely located properties in national parks that it decided to eliminate, even if the properties are not accessible by road and only seasonally accessible by water.[382] Overall, only 122 properties of the 40,000 screened have been transferred for homeless assistance in the program's 26-year history, with only 81 of these properties currently in use for homeless assistance.[383] It takes years of work to sell even one federal property in this painful process.

In addition to disposal process problems, the federal government struggles to figure out what it owns. GAO found that the federal government "continues to face challenges with the accuracy and consistency of the Federal

Real Property Profile (FRPP), causing the federal government to report inaccurate inventory and outcome information."[384] It is not surprising that the federal government cannot manage its real estate holdings when it cannot even measure them.

RECOVERY

Congress in conjunction with federal agencies needs to develop a better process for disposing of unused and unwanted federal property and could start by allowing agencies to have greater latitude to sell property and expedite the processes to do so. Congress should also require agencies to conduct a thorough, real property assessment and have a full and accessible federal property database. American families do not pay taxes every year so their government can buy and hoard property. They should be assured that when their government buys a building or property, it is necessary to fulfill an essential federal function.

For more information, please visit:
GSA: Real Property Disposal
GAO: Federal Real Property
CRS Report: Disposal of Unneeded Federal Buildings: Legislative Proposals in the 112th Congress

NLRB HATES SMALL BUSINESS

QUICK STATS

- ✗ **CONFERENCE:** Regulation
- ✗ **TEAM:** National Labor Relations Board
- ◯ **FUMBLE:** Lost jobs; stunted economy; devastated small businesses
- ◯ **HOW TO RECOVER THE BALL:** Pass the Protecting Local Business Opportunity Act, and rein in the NLRB with greater oversight

Americans love small businesses, especially locally owned franchises. Franchise employees—such as those at a fast food restaurant—are considered employed by the person who owns the local franchise, not the main company. That seems simple and straightforward, right?

Enter NLRB.

NLRB recently expanded the definition of joint employer through a rule that says any "indirect and unexercised control" also warrants classification as a joint employer. That means that all franchise employees—whether local or national—will be treated not as employees of the local small business but of the corporate entity. As a result, many more businesses will face a litany of obligations and liabilities they did not expect or want. In the words of dissenters of the decision, the new and improved arbitrary definition has the potential to "subject countless entities to unprecedented new joint-bargaining obligations that most do not even know they have, to potential liability for unfair labor practices and breaches of collective bargaining agreements, and to economic protest activity, including what have heretofore been unlawful secondary strikes, boycotts and picketing."[385]

So what does all this mean? Consider these hypotheticals. Steve of Ardmore, Oklahoma, lost his last job and turned to a temp agency to help him find new work. His agency used to work with a customer service call center to place temp workers who were eventually hired full-time by the call center. But under this new rule, the call center faces obligations under the new joint-employer standard and cannot take the risk of accepting temp workers. So Steve's agency cannot place him. Or what about Ann in Oklahoma City, who has successfully worked as a subcontractor for a construction business? Ann can no longer find work because the employers for whom she used to subcontract cannot take the risk of having subcontractors.[386] Who loses here? Real people.

RECOVERY

The majority of NLRB says that, "It is not the goal of joint-employer law to guarantee the freedom of employers to insulate themselves from their legal responsibility to workers,"[387] which is great as long as workers can actually find work. NLRB would have Americans believe that Steve and Ann are "law-school-exam hypothetical of doomsday scenarios."[388] Congress should disagree. S. 2015, the Protecting Local Business Opportunity Act, would codify the original joint-employer standard and relieve businesses of NLRB's unnecessary intrusion. Congress should pass this bill and also provide greater oversight of NLRB to prevent it from further overreach. Congress should encourage more small business, not force people to work for megacorporations.

For more information, please visit:
NLRB: Board Issues Decision in Browning-Ferris Industries
The Wall Street Journal: NLRB's Joint Employer Attack

CORN SQUEEZE-UMS FOR YOUR CAR

QUICK STATS

- ✗ **CONFERENCE:** Spending
- ✗ **TEAM:** Department of Agriculture
- ○ **FUMBLE:** $100 million in renewable energy research
- ○ **HOW TO RECOVER THE BALL:** Congress should stop forcing Americans to buy more of a product they do not want

Over the past six years, USDA spent $332 million on renewable energy research and recently decided to spend another $100 million.[389] On May 29, 2015, Agriculture Secretary Tom Vilsack announced USDA would invest up to $100 million in a Biofuels Infrastructure Partnership to make more renewable fuel options available to American consumers.[390] Specifically, USDA will administer competitive grants to match funding for state-led efforts to test and evaluate innovative and comprehensive approaches to market higher blends of renewable fuel (such as E15 and E85). Americans have access to gasoline for their cars, but USDA and EPA want Americans to buy more corn ethanol instead of gasoline.

Creating new, higher ethanol blends will require developing and installing new gas pumps that are equipped to handle such high levels of ethanol. Currently typical gas pumps can deliver fuel containing up to ten percent ethanol (E10) and no more.

USDA also incentivized more than 850 growers and landowners, farming nearly 48,000 acres, to establish and produce dedicated, non-food energy crops for delivery to energy conversion facilities. The $332 million invested over the last six years was used to accelerate research on renewable energy—from genomic research on bioenergy—from feedstock crops to development of biofuel conversion processes and cost-benefit estimates of renewable energy production. In comparison to the initial investment and efforts toward more renewable fuel sources, $100 million is just pocket change, right? Hard-working American taxpayers probably do not think so.

RECOVERY

Do American families, farmers, and manufacturing industries really want more options at the gas pump? Americans are already offered "environmentally friendly" vehicle and fuel options. Developing the infrastructure to utilize and maintain those fuel options will cost billions of dollars.

The RFS has been a regulatory disaster with missed deadlines, increased fuel costs, and confused consumers. Most vehicles on America's roads will void their warrenty if they use more than E10 gasoline for fuel. But that has not stopped EPA from trying to force them to use it. Environmental groups have now rejected increasing ethanol use because of the massive water requirements and increased ozone production. Congress should stop federal mandates on fuel options and allow the market to move low-cost energy to consumers. In many regions of the U.S., ethanol is very affordable; in some regions it is not affordable. The federal government must stop forcing taxpayers to subside ethanol everywhere.

For more information, please visit:
USDA: USDA to Invest Up to $100 Million to Boost Infrastructure for Renewable Fuel Use, Seeking to Double Number of Higher Blend Renewable Fuel Pumps
Agri-Pulse: USDA seeks to boost availability of E15, E85 at the pump

TAXING THE WORLD

QUICK STATS

✘ **CONFERENCE:** Regulation (sometimes known as taxes)
✘ **TEAM:** Department of the Treasury
○ **FUMBLE:** Highest corporate tax rate and an uncompetitive tax system
○ **HOW TO RECOVER THE BALL:** Reduce the corporate tax rate and transition toward a territorial tax system

The broken American corporate tax system is driving businesses and jobs out of the country in droves. In fact the U.S. corporate tax system has become so uncompetitive with the rest of the world that Treasury has issued regulations to attempt to keep US corporations here against their will, essentially holding them hostage. This is a consequence of Congress' inability to take up and pass a long-overdue overhaul of the tax code.

Currently the U.S. has the highest corporate tax rate in the developed world.[391] With a statutory rate of 39 percent (combined federal and state), the U.S. is ten percent above the Organization for Economic Co-Operation and Development (OECD) average.[392] To make matters worse, the U.S. is one of the few countries, and the only one in the G-7, to deploy a worldwide system.[393] There are two ways that countries tax corporate income earned out of the country: worldwide and territorial. In a worldwide tax system, any income earned overseas is still subject to taxes under the home countries' corporate tax code (most, including the U.S., allow the deferral of income earned abroad until it is returned home). A territorial system only taxes income earned domestically at the corporate rate while any income earned overseas is taxed at the rate of the country in which it is earned.

In recent years the combination of the high tax rate and punitive worldwide tax system has sent a string of U.S. companies fleeing for safer waters. Once a wonky term reserved for corporate tax attorneys, lately the word *inversion* has become a regular part of our country's vernacular. While the process and dynamics are complex, put simply, an inversion occurs when a U.S. company merges with an overseas company and reincorporates in that foreign country to take advantage of a better tax system. To put it even more simply, the uncompetitive American tax code forces companies to evacuate the U.S., taking jobs and taxable revenues with them. The tax code has turned many American corporations into sitting ducks waiting to be purchased by foreign competitors.

An analysis of the roughly $24.5 trillion in cross-border mergers and acquisition transactions over the last decade determined that if the U.S. had a 25-percent tax rate, "US companies would have acquired $590 billion in cross-border assets over the past 10-years instead of losing $179 billion in assets (a net shift of $769 billion in assets from foreign countries to the U.S.)."[394] Moreover, the report estimates that the U.S. would have kept 1,300 companies here if the tax code had a 25 percent rate.

While taxes are not the only—or even the top—consideration for companies looking to merge, the advantage countries with competitive tax systems have when deciding where to incorporate often provides a marginal advantage to put those countries at the top of the list. The merger between Burger King and Tim Hortons is a perfect example of the lack of competitiveness of the U.S. tax system. Burger King and Tim Hortons was a merger of similarly positioned companies that was driven by fundamental business synergies between the two companies—it made sense regardless of any tax implications. However, when it came time to determine where the new company would be domiciled, the U.S. was never even considered because of our tax system. If they would have domiciled in the U.S., the newly merged company would have lost about $5.5 billion in value over the first five years alone. Ultimately Canada was chosen as the headquarters location because of the favorable tax code.[395]

RECOVERY

The current U.S. corporate tax system inhibits American companies from competing globally and impedes their ability to increase domestic investment and jobs for American families. To restore competitiveness in an increasingly globalized economy, Congress must enact corporate tax reform that lowers the corporate tax rate and transitions the U.S. toward a territorial system. The Administration should stop trying to beat up companies when they move overseas and should start working with Congress to prevent the reason for their departure.

For more information, please visit:
CRS Report: The Corporate Income Tax System: Overview and Options for Reform
OECD: Corporate Income Tax Rate table
United States Senate Permanent Subcommittee on Investigations Committee on Homeland Security and Governmental Affairs: Impact of the U.S. Tax Code on the Market for Corporate Control and Jobs Report

IF IT IS WORTH DOING ONCE, IT IS WORTH DOING EIGHT TIMES

QUICK STATS

- ✘ **CONFERENCE:** Overlapping federal inspections
- ✘ **TEAM:** Multiple Agencies
- ○ **FUMBLE:** Duplicative laboratory inspection rules
- ○ **HOW TO RECOVER THE BALL:** Agencies should coordinate to avoid duplicative, burdensome inspections

Most families agree the scientific laboratories that develop the pesticides farmers use to grow their crops and ultimately feed American families should be thoroughly inspected to ensure they follow all applicable rules and laws. However, multiple federal agencies should not waste taxpayer money to duplicate inspection efforts.

In one particular instance, GAO found that from 2005-2012, both EPA and FDA conducted eight total inspections of the same pesticide laboratory for compliance with good laboratory practices.[396] Moreover EPA and FDA failed to renew an interagency agreement in 2004 that facilitated interagency coordination on the inspections of pesticide laboratories, which could have prevented the burdensome, overlapping inspections. A representative from one of the laboratories told GAO that some of the information in the toxicology studies FDA officials examined during a 2011 inspection could have been shared with EPA officials to increase efficiency.[397]

RECOVERY

Here is a new idea: EPA and FDA should work together. All federal agencies should coordinate inspections to save taxpayer money and relieve our country's laboratories of the burden of additional, unnecessary inspections. American scientists are best able to produce chemicals that are safe for families when they do not have to waste time and resources going through duplicative federal inspections. If agencies cannot accomplish this on their own, Congress should design a process that easily allows agencies to share information and ensure activities do not directly overlap with the actions of another agency.

For more information, please visit:
GAO: 2015 Annual Report: Additional Opportunities to Reduce Fragmentation, Overlap, and Duplication and Achieve Other Financial Benefits

FOOL ME ONCE, SHAME ON YOU; FOOL ME TWICE, SHAME ON ME

QUICK STATS

- ✘ **CONFERENCE:** Spending
- ✘ **TEAM:** Congress
- ◯ **FUMBLE:** Creating fake savings in federal spending
- ◯ **HOW TO RECOVER THE BALL:** Congress should end the use of budget gimmicks

For most Americans balancing the family budget is fairly simple—income earned minus expenses paid. It is not that straightforward for the federal government. For years Congress has used an array of budget gimmicks to create fake savings in one area of federal spending to justify more debt spending somewhere else. These gimmicks have been used recently to pay for things like highway funding[398] and trade preferences bills.[399]

One method to accomplish the gimmicks is called changes in mandatory spending, or "CHIMPS," which are provisions in spending bills that artificially reduce spending in future years so Congress can spend the money this year. If Congress only did that once, it might be okay. But Congress actually uses the same "savings" year after year even though the money was actually spent years ago.

Another example is pension smoothing, which lowers the required contributions to pension plans by employers. This practice produces more taxable income for the employer, which results in more revenue for the federal government. But it also produces a less stable pension plan in the future.

A final example is corporate tax shifting, which is used to satisfy budget constraints that prohibit legislation from increasing the deficit over five and ten years. Under this gimmick the amount of corporate tax owed is higher in the third quarter of the year and then less in the fourth quarter. In the end the same amount of money comes to the federal government—only the timing for when it comes is shifted. No money is saved. It is simply shifted one month beyond the budget plan.

RECOVERY

Using accounting gimmicks to create fake savings is unacceptable.. Family budgets do not operate like this, and neither should the American government's budget. The U.S. cannot become fiscally responsible if the federal government is not honest about how to reduce deficit spending. No company could legally use any of these accounting gimmicks, and the federal government should not be able to use them either.

For more information, please visit:
Trade Preferences Extension Act of 2015
Politico: Faking It
The Wall Street Journal: Welcome to the World of "Pension Smoothing"

REGULATIONS CRUSH SMALL, COMMUNITY BANKS

QUICK STATS

- ✘ **CONFERENCE:** Regulation
- ✘ **TEAM:** Multiple agencies
- ○ **FUMBLE:** $895 billion by 2025
- ○ **HOW TO RECOVER THE BALL:** The Financial Regulatory Improvement Act

If Dodd-Frank's goal was to put a check on "big" banks and bolster small community banks, the 2,300-page law certainly missed the mark. The law created a total of 390 rules and regulations, and as of September 30, 2015, a total of 249 have been finalized—with 58 remaining proposed and 83 yet to be proposed.[400] The American Action Forum estimates that by 2025 Dodd-Frank will cost the American economy a staggering $895 billion.[401]

New community banks, which give American families the opportunity to invest in a small local bank that will in turn invest in their local community, have essentially stopped opening across the country in part because of Dodd-Frank's enormous costs. A Federal Reserve Board report found that "from 1990 to 2008, more than 2,000 new banks were formed," while "from 2009 to 2013 only seven new banks were formed."[402]

Small banks across the country struggle to comply with Dodd-Frank's complex rules. Families rely on their community banks for mortgages to buy their first homes or for important financing to open small businesses. If banks continue to close down or focus only on federal compliance, where will families and small business owners turn? In just one of countless examples, the *Washington Post* reports that a local DC-area bank was forced to expand its compliance team sevenfold to 35 full-time, non-revenue-generating employees since Dodd-Frank's enactment in 2010.[403]

RECOVERY

Recognizing the urgent need to help local banks, the U.S. Senate Committee on Banking, Housing and Urban Affairs's Financial Regulatory Improvement Act will fix many of Dodd-Frank's requirements by freeing small banks from complying with new regulations that were intended for larger banks. Congress must pass common-sense legislation like this to free community banks from Dodd-Frank's shackles and allow them to provide American small businesses and families with crucial local financing.

For more information, please visit:
American Action Forum: The Growth Consequences of Dodd-Frank
Federal Reserve: Where Are All the New Banks? The Role of Regulatory Burden in New Charter Creation
The Washington Post: Four years into Dodd-Frank, local banks say this is the year they'll feel the most impact
Davis Polk: Dodd-Frank Progress Report

DISABILITY IS ONLY FOR THE DISABLED

QUICK STATS

- ✗ **CONFERENCE:** Regulation
- ✗ **TEAM:** Social Security Administration
- ○ **FUMBLE:** $1.2 Million
- ○ **HOW TO RECOVER THE BALL:** SSA should inspect what they expect

The U.S. has always been a generous nation, especially for those in greatest need. Individuals and families in need can always count on a friend, neighbor, or their fellow Americans to step up and lend a helping hand.

The Disability Insurance (DI) program of the SSA requires anyone on DI to regularly undergo a Continuing Disability Review (CDR) to ensure he or she is still disabled and qualifies for benefits. The requirement should not be different for child recipients, especially as they transition to adulthood. Recently the number of conducted reviews dropped significantly, even though the number of children qualified to receive assistance grew dramatically. From 2000 to 2013, the amount of money spent on Social Security Insurance rose from $33 billion to $57 billion per year.[404] However, from 2000 to 2011, the number of reviews fell from more than 150,000 to around 45,000 per year.[405]

RECOVERY

Congress should work with SSA to eliminate the backlog of CDRs. It should also put in place a mandatory review for every three years a person receives assistance through SSI to ensure reviews are conducted at least that often. The safety net should be proected for the disabled by ensuring that only the truly disabled are in the program.

For more information, please visit:
CATO Institute: Supplemental Security Income: A Costly and Troubled Welfare Program
GAO: Supplemental Security Income: Better Management Oversight Needed for Children's Benefits

MOTOR MANDATES

QUICK STATS

- ✗ **CONFERENCE:** Regulation
- ✗ **TEAM:** Environmental Protection Agency
- ○ **FUMBLE:** Requirement to blend biofuels into the gasoline supply
- ○ **HOW TO RECOVER THE BALL:** Eliminate regulations that drive up gasoline prices and risk destroying car engines

The federal government requires Americans to put corn in their gas tanks. Originating in a 2005 law (and subsequent 2007 revision), the Renewable Fuel Standard (RFS) requires blenders (those who prepare the gasoline that goes into cars) to incorporate a congressionally specified volume of biofuels.[406] Most of the mandate is met with ethanol derived from corn, although in the future much more of it is required to be met with fuels derived from feedstocks like straw and wood byproducts—a fuel that so far has failed to be made in volumes anyone can afford, anywhere near those required under the law.[407]

Beyond the not-so-minor detail that one of the required fuels does not exist in large enough quantities to meet the mandate, there are many other problems with the EPA-administered program that leads to higher prices at the pump. Prime among them is the constant threat of hitting the blend wall: motor engines, especially those in older cars, can only use gasoline with an ethanol content below ten percent or risk damage to the engine. If engine damage on a new or old car results from the use of a fuel with a higher ethanol content, the manufacturer may void the car's warranty by forcing consumers to cover the cost of repairs.[408] Blenders are aware of this risk and have, until now, managed to keep ethanol content below ten percent. However, one of the ways they are able to do this is to purchase compliance credits instead of meeting the requirement when meeting the mandate would cause them to breach the blend wall. As the mandated volume increases over the next seven years, compliance through credits will become more likely. Ultimately, what this may mean for American families is a higher price at the gas pump.[409]

The policy has not yielded great results for environmental protection either. Research has shown that corn ethanol is actually worse for air quality than gasoline, as it contributes to higher levels of ground ozone.[410] Coincidentally, EPA also sets limits for how high ozone levels may be. This means EPA is responsible for a regulation that increases a pollutant and then another to require a decrease of the same pollutant.

RECOVERY

The original intent of the RFS was admirable: to support American energy independence and protect the environment. Now, ten years later, foreign oil constitutes the lowest percentage of total American oil consumption since 1985 because of new American energy discoveries.[411] It is time to do away with a mandate that fails to meet its goals while imposing higher consumer costs for families. Corn ethanol in small quantities is an acceptable fuel, but why artificially increase American use when it solves nothing?

For more information, please visit:
U.S. Energy Information Administration: Frequently Asked Questions
CRS Report: Renewable Fuel Standard (RFS): Overview and Issues
CRS Report: Intermediate-Level Blends of Ethanol in Gasoline, and the Ethanol "Blend Wall"
Nature Geoscience: Reduction in Local Ozone Levels in Urban Sao Paulo due to a Shift from Ethanol to Gasoline Use

WHY COMMUNICATION MATTERS

QUICK STATS

- ✘ **CONFERENCE:** Regulation
- ✘ **TEAM:** All federal departments
- ○ **FUMBLE:** Agencies often fail to consult with public prior to issuance of regulations
- ○ **HOW TO RECOVER THE BALL:** Implement the Early Participation in Regulations Act.

Federal agencies can work together with stakeholders to develop appropriate and cost-effective regulations. When agencies provide advance notice of rulemaking to businesses and other impacted entities, positive results generally follow. That is how the process should work. However, too often agencies fail to work with the public early in the process, which can mean the only choice is the preferred agency-developed solution. In other words, if agencies do not talk to the public about a rule, it is easier for the agency to ignore the public's interests and just use the rule the agency originally wanted.

Photo: Shutterstock

In general current law only requires notices of proposed rulemaking, which insufficiently capture the beginning of the rulemaking process because agency staff frequently have already laid out a preferred path at that point, before hearing from the general public. Agency regulations often end up burdening stakeholders in ways that agencies might not have predicted. This could be avoided if the public could provide comments for common-sense solutions.

Abraham Lincoln acknowledged the need for thorough early planning and once quipped, if given "six hours to chop down a tree… I will spend the first four sharpening the axe." Everyday Americans, from mechanics to small farmers, know how regulations affect the bottom lines of businesses, and regulators should take their valuable input into account. One recent case highlighted the importance of early engagement with stakeholders when the Department of Labor's Office of Federal Contract Compliance Programs (OFCCP) developed a better regulation as a result of the public's early involvement.[412]

A detailed 2015 U.S. Chamber of Commerce report on labor regulatory initiatives outlines how the Chamber proactively commented on an advance notice of OFCCP's regulatory proposal to strengthen affirmative action requirements under the Rehabilitation Act. The Chamber was concerned about five costly elements of OFCCP's proposed rule regarding numerical targets for employers that would likely do little to increase the hiring of individuals with disabilities. In this instance

OFCCP agreed with the Chamber and adopted three improvements to the final rule, which eliminated approximately $250 million of the original rule's estimated first-year costs and still increased the hiring of individuals with disabilities.[413]

RECOVERY

To improve the regulatory system and ensure regulators follow this regulation's example, Congress should pass S.1820, the Early Participation in Regulations Act of 2015. S. 1820 would require agencies to publish an advance notice of proposed rulemaking for major rules. This will provide greater regulatory predictability to businesses and enable greater communication between agencies and the public.

For more information, please visit:
Federal Register: Affirmative Action and Nondiscrimination Obligations of Contractors and Subcontractors Regarding Individuals With Disabilities
U.S. Chamber of Commerce: Key Labor, Employment, and Immigration, Regulatory Initiatives in the Obama Administration

OUT-OF-CONTROL OZONE

QUICK STATS

- ✗ **CONFERENCE:** Regulation
- ✗ **TEAM:** Environmental Protection Agency
- ○ **FUMBLE:** Costly changes to the National Ambient Air Quality Standards for ground-level ozone prior to full implementation of the previous standard
- ○ **HOW TO RECOVER THE BALL:** Allow sufficient time to meet existing standards before considering making them more stringent

In October 2015 EPA finalized a rule to lower the National Ambient Air Quality Standards (NAAQS) for ground-level ozone (the primary component of smog) from the current 75 parts per billion (ppb) standard to 70 ppb. This seemingly small change comes with a high cost. A conservative estimate provided by EPA calculated the cost at $1.4 billion annually for all states except California.[414]

The new standard is being finalized despite the prior standard not yet achieving full implementation. As recently as October 2015, 224 counties spanning 25 states were classified in "non-attainment," meaning their ozone levels exceeded the current 75-ppb standard. This area affects many people because these 224 countries in non-attainment account for about 40 percent of all Americans.[415] The change has practical implications for any business looking to grow and for workers looking for jobs. If an area is not compliant with the standard, businesses that may contribute to increasing the ozone level would need to find a way to offset the increase or may simply not be allowed to take on new projects.[416] The need to comply inevitably imposes costs on expansion, so growth becomes harder financially every time EPA tightens the standard. By the way, EPA's ethanol mandate for fuel increases ozone. So EPA's own rules help contribute to ozone issues.

RECOVERY

Under current law EPA is required to re-evaluate the ozone standard every five years, and update it as appropriate. This timeline is simply not long enough for areas to achieve attainment and to truly assess whether the existing standard is sufficient before EPA must once again revisit the rule. Congress should develop a better, long-term approach that will provide stability for states and businesses. Until that time Congress should stop EPA from lowering the NAAQS standards to a level most communities cannot attain.

For more information, please visit:
CRS Report: Ozone Air Quality Standards: EPA's 2015 Revision
CRS Report: Clean Air Act: A Summary of the Act and Its Major Requirements

THE LARGEST THEFT OF FEDERAL DATA IN HISTORY

QUICK STATS

- ✘ **CONFERENCE:** Regulation
- ✘ **TEAM:** Office of Personnel Management
- ○ **FUMBLE:** Loss of personal data of 22 million federal employees
- ○ **HOW TO RECOVER THE BALL:** Protect passwords and increase cybersecurity

OPM provides administrative and personnel services to the federal workforce nationwide. To do that it maintains private personal information—including Social Security numbers—as part of its employment records on all past and present federal workers and on those who have applied for federal service. OPM also possesses personal information on federal employees' family members and contractors if that information was included by a federal worker filing to obtain a security clearance. Unfortunately, OPM failed to heed multiple warnings over several years from the IG to beef up its security systems, even though OPM subcontractors were also victims of major cyberattacks.[417]

As a result OPM announced on June 4, 2015, that its data systems had been breached, resulting in the potential exposure of an estimated 4.2 million federal employees. On July 9, 2015, OPM announced a second cyber breach that had exposed the personal information of at least 17.9 million additional federal employees, their families, and federal contractors. The breaches were traced back to hacks that occurred between May and December 2014, and they exposed the federal government—and American families—to untold liabilities. The breaches amount to what experts call "among the largest known thefts of government data in history"[418] by compromising the personal information of at least 22.1 million American citizens.

To begin repairing the damage, on June 2, 2015, OPM spent almost $21 million for a credit-monitoring services contract and insurance coverage. The preliminary contract insures federal workers up to $1 million—but only for one year of coverage.[419] On September 1, 2015, OPM awarded an additional contract worth $133 million for three additional years of credit and identity monitoring and insurance services for affected federal workers. It is too early to say whether these measures were sufficient to protect federal workers from identity theft as a result of the breach—after all, the attack's perpetrators could use, sell, or dump the stolen information at any time. As a result major federal employee unions sued OPM for failure to protect their members' personal information, seeking lifetime credit monitoring.[420]

The federal government still does not know—and may not know for years to come—the extent of the damage done by the massive OPM breach. The monetary damage alone could be astronomical. But perhaps even more troubling has been OPM's failure to heed multiple warnings to fortify its security systems that house federal workers' personal information, which demonstrates a fundamental failure by the federal government to protect the identities of its own workers and their families. *That* harm is irreparable.

RECOVERY

As a result of the OPM breach, on October 27, 2015, the Senate passed the Cybersecurity Information Sharing Act of 2015 (CISA), which will ensure better communication about and preparation for cybersecurity threats across the federal government and private sectors. Specifically CISA directs the Director of National Intelligence, Secretaries of Homeland Security and Defense, and the Attorney General to develop procedures for sharing information on cybersecurity threats and best practices to address those threats.[421] By requiring the federal government to "utilize security controls to protect against unauthorized access or acquisitions," this bill will require the federal government to fix its inconsistent and vulnerable sensitive information safeguards.

OPM could also start by directing employees to change passwords more frequently and requiring higher authentication standards. A breach of this magnitude touches millions of American families and is a violation of the trust Americans place in the federal government. OPM must ensure it never happens again.

For more information, please visit:
The Wall Street Journal: U.S. Suspects Hackers in China Breached About 4 Million People's Records, Officials Say
The Hill: Largest federal workers union sues OPM over breach
FedSmith: OPM Releases New List of FAQs on Data Breach
FCW: Exclusive: The OPM breach details you haven't seen

TOUCHDOWN!

The purpose of this book is to highlight the work needed to make the federal government more fiscally responsible and less burdensome on the American people. It is not intended to collect dust on a shelf, sit in somene's email to wait for later, or just receive honorable mention in the history books. It is truly a guide for next year—to guide us while we work through the federal budget, to encourage federal oversight, and to remind those of us who work in the federal government that we must be responsible servants of the people.

This book is also a way for the American people to judge their elected officials and their government. We identified 100 problems. Over the next year, our charge is to find solutions to these problems and prevent them from happening again—to turn these "fumbles" into "touchdowns," or examples of the government getting the job done right. Next year's edition of *Federal Fumbles* will have a list of these touchdowns so American taxpayers can see the improvements made in their government.

Fortunately there are already a few examples from the last year or so where we found solutions to waste and duplication in the federal government. Here are some examples:

Duplication has long been a problem in the federal government. Between 2011 and 2014, GAO highlighted 1,100 duplicative federal programs that cost billions each year. These reports have helped Congress and the Administration eliminate some duplicative programs and save more than $10 billion. More work needs to be done.[422]

DOD has already made advancements in consolidating some medical services with the creation of the Defense Health Agency in 2013. GAO had previously recommended DOD realign medical services to remove duplication and unify the command structure. DOD estimated at the time that the reforms would save $46.5 million a year. Way to go, DOD.[423]

One area of reform in which DOJ has found success is spending on conferences. In 2010 DOJ spent around $92 million on 1,740 conferences or events. After DOJ's IG recommended reforms to bring these numbers down, in 2014 DOJ spent less than $20 million on 445 events. These numbers can always be lower, but DOJ has made progress. Well done.[424]

ENDNOTES

[1] Sopko, John. "DOD's Compressed Natural Gas Filling Station in Afghanistan: An Ill-Conceived $43 Million Project." Special Investigator General for Afghanistan Reconstruction. 22 Oct. 2015. 4. <https://www.sigar.mil/pdf/special%20projects/SIGAR-16-2-SP.pdf >.

[2] Sopko, John. "DOD's Compressed Natural Gas Filling Station in Afghanistan: An Ill-Conceived $43 Million Project." Special Investigator General for Afghanistan Reconstruction. 22 Oct. 2015. 4. <https://www.sigar.mil/pdf/special%20projects/SIGAR-16-2-SP.pdf >.

[3] Sopko, John. "DOD's Compressed Natural Gas Filling Station in Afghanistan: An Ill-Conceived $43 Million Project." Special Investigator General for Afghanistan Reconstruction. 22 Oct. 2015. 5. <https://www.sigar.mil/pdf/special%20projects/SIGAR-16-2-SP.pdf >.

[4] Sopko, John. "DOD's Compressed Natural Gas Filling Station in Afghanistan: An Ill-Conceived $43 Million Project." Special Investigator General for Afghanistan Reconstruction. 22 Oct. 2015. 6. <https://www.sigar.mil/pdf/special%20projects/SIGAR-16-2-SP.pdf >.

[5] Sopko, John. "DOD's Compressed Natural Gas Filling Station in Afghanistan: An Ill-Conceived $43 Million Project." Special Investigator General for Afghanistan Reconstruction. 22 Oct. 2015. 6. <https://www.sigar.mil/pdf/special%20projects/SIGAR-16-2-SP.pdf >.

[6] Sopko, John. "DOD's Compressed Natural Gas Filling Station in Afghanistan: An Ill-Conceived $43 Million Project." Special Investigator General for Afghanistan Reconstruction. 22 Oct. 2015. 4. <https://www.sigar.mil/pdf/special%20projects/SIGAR-16-2-SP.pdf >.

[7] Pomerleau, Kyle. "Tax Freedom Day 2015 is April 24." Tax Foundation. 30 March 2015. <http://taxfoundation.org/article/tax-freedom-day-2015-april-24th>.

[8] "Creative Placemaking Guidelines and Report Launched by NEA." Virginia Commission for the Arts. 21 May 2015. <http://www.arts.virginia.gov/2015_5.html>.

[9] "(New) Synetic Theater." Virginia Commission for the Arts. <http://www.arts.virginia.gov/PATD_T_Synetic-Theater.html>.

[10] "2013-2014 Grants Awarded as of July 2013." Virginia Commission for the Arts. 1 July 2013. <http://www.arts.virginia.gov/about/pdf/grants1314.pdf>.

[11] "Grants Awarded June 2011 for Fiscal Year 2011-2012." Virginia Commission for the Arts. June 2011. <http://www.arts.virginia.gov/grants/pdf/GRANTS2012.pdf >.

[12] "2012 – 2013 Grants Awarded as of July 1, 2012." Virginia Commission for the Arts. <http://www.arts.virginia.gov/grants/pdf/12-13%20VCA%20Grants.pdf>.

[13] "Grant Awards." Virginia Commision for the Arts. <http://www.arts.virginia.gov/Copy%20of%20VCA%202016%20Grant%20Awards.pdf>.

[14] Bovard, James. "A Silenced Shakespeare in Washington." *The Wall Street Journal.* 13 July 2015. <http://www.wsj.com/articles/a-silenced-shakespeare-in-washington-1436825550>.

[15] Sherlock, Molly. "Electricity Production from Renewable Energies." Congressional Research Service. 14 July 2015. PDF 2. <http://nationalaglawcenter.org/wp-content/uploads/assets/crs/R43453.pdf>.

[16] Brown, Phillip. "U.S. Renewable Electricity: How Does Wind Generation Impact Competitive Power Markets?" Congressional Research Service. 7 Nov. 2012. PDF 2. <http://www.lankford.senate.gov/imo/media/doc/US%20Renewable%20Electricity%20How%20Does%20Wind%20Generation%20Impact%20Competitive%20Power%20Markets.pdf>.

[17] "Oklahoma: State Profile and Energy Estimates." Energy Information Administration. <http://www.eia.gov/state/?sid=OK>.

[18] "Most States have Renewable Portfolio Standards." Energy Information Agency. 3 Feb. 2012. <http://www.eia.gov/todayinenergy/detail.cfm?id=4850>.

[19] Sherlock, Molly F. "The Renewable Electricity Production Tax Credit: In Brief." Congressional Research Service. 14 July 2015. 7. <http://www.lankford.senate.gov/imo/media/doc/The%20Renewable%20Electricity%20Production%20Tax%20Credit%20In%20Brief.pdf>.

[20] Roth, John. "Management Alert – ICE San Pedro Service Processing Center." Department of Homeland Security. 11 Dec. 2014. 2-3. <https://www.oig.dhs.gov/assets/Mga/OIG_mga-121114.pdf>.

[21] Roth, John. "Management Alert – ICE San Pedro Service Processing Center." Department of Homeland Security. 11 Dec. 2014. 1. <https://www.oig.dhs.gov/assets/Mga/OIG_mga-121114.pdf>.

[22] "Follow-up to Management Alert – ICE San Pedro Service Processing Center." Department of Homeland Security. 9 July 2015. 3. <https://www.oig.dhs.gov/assets/Mgmt/2015/OIG-15-112-Jul15.pdf>.
[23] "Follow-up to Management Alert – ICE San Pedro Service Processing Center." Department of Homeland Security. 9 July 2015. 3. <https://www.oig.dhs.gov/assets/Mgmt/2015/OIG-15-112-Jul15.pdf>.
[24] "Follow-up to Management Alert – ICE San Pedro Service Processing Center." Department of Homeland Security. 9 July 2015. 3. <https://www.oig.dhs.gov/assets/Mgmt/2015/OIG-15-112-Jul15.pdf>.
[25] "Follow-up to Management Alert – ICE San Pedro Service Processing Center." Department of Homeland Security. 9 July 2015. 3. <https://www.oig.dhs.gov/assets/Mgmt/2015/OIG-15-112-Jul15.pdf>.
[26] Brown, Kay. "School Lunch: Modifications Needed to Some of the New Nutrition Standards. Government Accountability Office. 27 June 2013. 10. <http://www.gao.gov/assets/660/655543.pdf>.
[27] Brown, Kay. "School Lunch: Modifications Needed to Some of the New Nutrition Standards." Government Accountability Office. 27 June 2013. <http://www.gao.gov/assets/660/655543.pdf>.
[28] Moran, Jerry. "S.1800 - Agriculture, Rural Development, Food and Drug Administration, and Related Agencies Appropriations Act, 2016," Introduced 16 July 2015. <https://www.congress.gov/bill/114th-congress/senate-bill/1800?q=%7B%22search%22%3A%5B%22fiscal+year+2016+Agriculture+Appropriations+Bill%22%5D%7D&resultIndex=16>.
[29] Jones, Yvonne. "Federal Paid Administrative Leave: Additional Guidance Needed to Improve OPM Data." Government Accountability Office. Oct. 2014. 23-26. United States Government Accountability Office. <http://www.gao.gov/assets/670/666566.pdf>.
[30] Jones, Yvonne. "Federal Paid Administrative Leave: Additional Guidance Needed to Improve OPM Data." Government Accountability Office. Oct. 2014. 23-26. United States Government Accountability Office. <http://www.gao.gov/assets/670/666566.pdf>.
[31] "Efficiency." Merriam-Webster. <http://www.merriam-webster.com/dictionary/efficient>.
[32] "Energy Conservation Programs: Standards for Residential Dishwashers." Regulations. 19 Dec. 2014. <http://www.regulations.gov/#!documentDetail;D=EERE-2014-BT-STD-0021-0007>.
[33] "Appliance Industry Warns Federal Dishwasher Regs Would Lead to Dirty Dishes." *Fox News.* 20 July 2015. <http://www.foxnews.com/politics/2015/07/20/federal-dishwasher-proposals-upset-appliance-industry-conservatives/>.
[34] Cama, Timothy. "Industry Rails Against Obama's Dishwasher Rules." 20 July 2015. <http://thehill.com/policy/energy-environment/248385-industry-rails-against-obamas-dishwasher-rules>.
[35] "Project Information." National Institutes of Health. <https://projectreporter.nih.gov/project_info_history.cfm?aid=8836575&icde=25541060>.
[36] Wipfli, Brad, Ryan Olson, and Melanie Koren. "Weight Loss Maintenance Among SHIFT Pilot Study Participants 30-Months Post-Intervention." Jan 2013. <http://www.ncbi.nlm.nih.gov/pmc/articles/PMC3547666/>.
[37] Wipfli, Brad, Ryan Olson, and Melanie Koren. "Weight Loss Maintenance Among SHIFT Pilot Study Participants 30-Months Post-Intervention." Jan 2013. <http://www.ncbi.nlm.nih.gov/pmc/articles/PMC3547666/>.
[38] Wipfli, Brad, Ryan Olson, and Melanie Koren. "Weight Loss Maintenance Among SHIFT Pilot Study Participants 30-Months Post-Intervention." Jan 2013. <http://www.ncbi.nlm.nih.gov/pmc/articles/PMC3547666/>.
[39] Wipfli, Brad, Ryan Olson, and Melanie Koren. "Weight Loss Maintenance Among SHIFT Pilot Study Participants 30-Months Post-Intervention." Jan 2013. <http://www.ncbi.nlm.nih.gov/pmc/articles/PMC3547666/>.
[40] Wipfli, Brad, Ryan Olson, and Melanie Koren. "Weight Loss Maintenance Among SHIFT Pilot Study Participants 30-Months Post-Intervention." Jan 2013. <http://www.ncbi.nlm.nih.gov/pmc/articles/PMC3547666/>.
[41] "Project Information." National Institutes of Health. <https://projectreporter.nih.gov/project_info_history.cfm?aid=8836575&icde=25541060>.
[42] Goodlatte, Bob and Chuck Grassley. "Goodlatte and Grassley Press Homeland Security Secretary for Swift Action on Sanctuary Jurisdictions." Press Release. 6 Oct. 2015. <http://judiciary.house.gov/index.cfm/2015/10/goodlatte-and-grassley-press-homeland-security-secretary-for-swift-action-on-sanctuary-jurisdictions>.
[43] "Coastal California Gnatcatcher Habitat Use Study and Population Surveys at Marine Corps Air Station Miramar, California." Grants. 6 Aug. 2015. <http://www.grants.gov/web/grants/view-opportunity.html?oppId=278326>.
[44] "Inpatient Hospital Reviews." Centers for Medicare & Medicaid Services. 26 Oct. 2015 <https://www.cms.gov/research-statistics-data-and-systems/monitoring-programs/medicare-ffs-compliance-programs/medical-review/inpatienthospitalreviews.html>.
[45] Schoffstall, Joe. "CMS' Secretive Settlement." *The Washington Free Beacon.* 2 July 2015. <http://freebeacon.com/issues/cms-secretive-settlement/>.
[46] "Hearing to Receive Testimony on Counter-ISIL Strategy." Committee on Armed Services. 7 July 2015. 19. <http://www.armed-services.senate.gov/imo/media/doc/15-61%20-%207-7-15.pdf>.

[47] "Statement on Syria." Department of Defense. 9 Oct. 2015. <http://www.defense.gov/News/News-Releases/News-Release-View/Article/622610/statement-on-syria?source=GovDelivery>.

[48] "National Endowment for the Arts FY 2015 Springs Grant Announcement."National Endowment for the Arts. 17 April 2015. 100. <https://www.arts.gov/sites/default/files/spring-2015-grant-announcement-discipline-list-revised.pdf>.

[49] Boehm, Mike. "Film Academy's Museum Gets $25,000 Grant from the NEA." *Los Angeles Times*. May 2015. <http://www.latimes.com/entertainment/arts/culture/la-et-cm-nea-grants-los-angeles-20150506-story.html>.

[50] Kilday, Gregg. "Academy Museum Fundraising Chief to Step Down." *The Hollywood Reporter*. 2 Oct. 2015. <http://www.hollywoodreporter.com/news/bill-kramer-motion-picture-museum-828825>.

[51] Kilday, Gregg. "Academy Museum Fundraising Chief to Step Down." *The Hollywood Reporter*. 2 Oct. 2015. <http://www.hollywoodreporter.com/news/bill-kramer-motion-picture-museum-828825>.

[52] "Return of Organization Exempt from Income Tax. Academy of Motion Picture Arts and Science. 8 May 2014. <http://www.guidestar.org/FinDocuments/2013/950/473/2013-950473280-0a6ee25a-9O.pdf>.

[53] "Mission and Goals." National Institutes of Health. 9 Apr. 2015. <http://www.nih.gov/about-nih/what-we-do/mission-goals>.

[54] "Project Information." National Institutes of Health. <https://projectreporter.nih.gov/project_info_description.cfm?aid=8809996&icde=25552654>.

[55] Starks, Tricia. "Cigarettes and Soviets: The Culture of Tobacco Use in Modern Russia." Grantome. <http://grantome.com/grant/NIH/G13-LM011893-01A1>. *See also*: <https://projectreporter.nih.gov/project_info_description.cfm?aid=8809996&icde=25552654&ddparam=&ddvalue=&ddsub=&cr=1&csb=default&cs=ASC>.

[56] Starks, Tricia. "Cigarettes and Soviets: The Culture of Tobacco Use in Modern Russia." Grantome. <http://grantome.com/grant/NIH/G13-LM011893-01A1>. *See also*: <https://projectreporter.nih.gov/project_info_description.cfm?aid=8809996&icde=25552654&ddparam=&ddvalue=&ddsub=&cr=1&csb=default&cs=ASC>.

[57] "Clinical Advances." National Institutes of Health. 7 Jan. 2015. 18. <https://history.nih.gov/about/timelines_research_advances.html>.

[58] 15 C.F.R. §272.1. <http://www.gpo.gov/fdsys/pkg/CFR-2011-title7-vol4/pdf/CFR-2011-title7-vol4-sec272-1.pdf>.

[59] "Additional Opportunities to Reduce Fragmentation, Overlap, and Duplication and Achieve Other Financial Benefits." Government Accountability Office. April 2015. 65. <http://www.gao.gov/assets/670/669613.pdf>.

[60] "Congressional Training." Department of State. 9 July 2014. <https://www.fbo.gov/index?s=opportunity&mode=form&id=2f542f87238f0626072bd402f6f6e638&tab=core&_cview=1>.

[61] McElhatton, Jim. "State Department Hires Testimony Coach to Prepare for Congressional Grillings." *The Washington Post*. 7 Aug. 2014. <http://www.washingtontimes.com/news/2014/aug/7/state-department-hires-testimony-coach-to-prepare-/?page=all>.

[62] McElhatton, Jim. "State Department Hires Testimony Coach to Prepare for Congressional Grillings." *The Washington Post*. 7 Aug. 2014. <http://www.washingtontimes.com/news/2014/aug/7/state-department-hires-testimony-coach-to-prepare-/?page=all>.

[63] McElhatton, Jim. "State Department Hires Testimony Coach to Prepare for Congressional Grillings." *The Washington Post*. 7 Aug. 2014. <http://www.washingtontimes.com/news/2014/aug/7/state-department-hires-testimony-coach-to-prepare-/?page=all>.

[64] "Blurred Lines: A Media Ethics Course for Indian Journalists." Grants – Department of State. 7 July 2015. <http://www.grants.gov/web/grants/view-opportunity.html?oppId=277682>.

[65] "Blurred Lines: A Media Ethics Course for Indian Journalists." Grants – Department of State, 7 July 2015. <http://www.grants.gov/web/grants/view-opportunity.html?oppId=277682>.

[66] "Food Labeling; Nutrition Labeling of Standard Menu Items in Restaurants and Similar Retail Food Establishments; Calorie Labeling of Articles of Food in Vending Machines; Final Rule." Federal Register. 1 Dec. 2014. <http://www.gpo.gov/fdsys/pkg/FR-2014-12-01/pdf/2014-27833.pdf>.

[67] Devaney, Tim. "FDA Rolls out ObamaCare Menu Regs." *The Hill*. 24 Nov. 2014. <http://thehill.com/regulation/healthcare/225250-fda-rolls-out-obamacare-menu-labeling-regs>.

[68] McMorris Rodgers, Cathy. "H.R.2017 - Common Sense Nutrition Disclosure Act of 2015." Introduced 23 Apr. 2015. <https://www.congress.gov/bill/114th-congress/house-bill/2017/cosponsors?q=%7B%22search%22%3A%5B%22%5C%22hr2017%5C%22%22%5D%7D&resultIndex=1>.

[69] "Regulated Businesses (Licensing and Registration)." Department of Agriculture. 30 June 2015. <https://www.aphis.usda.gov/wps/portal/banner/help?urile=wcm%3apath%3a%2Faphis_content_library%2Fsa_our_focus%2Fsa_animal_welfare%2Fsa_awa%2Fct_awa_regulated_businesses>.

[70] "USDA Herding Internet's Celebrity Llamas out of the Spotlight, Owners Say." *The Guardian*. 28 March 2015. <http://www.theguardian.com/us-news/2015/mar/28/usda-llamas-license-owners-bub-bullis-karen-freund>.
[71] Johnson, Charles Michael. "Security Assistance: Taxpayer Funds Spent on Equipment That Was Never Shipped to Yemen." Government Accountability Office. July 2015. 10. <http://www.gao.gov/assets/680/671412.pdf>.
[72] "Congressional Budget Justification: Foreign Operations." Department of State. 2016. 213. <http://www.state.gov/documents/organization/238222.pdf>.
[73] "Al-Qaeda in the Arabian Peninsula." Council on Foreign Relations. 19 June 2015. <http://www.cfr.org/yemen/al-qaeda-arabian-peninsula-aqap/p9369>.
[74] Johnson, Charles Michael. "Security Assistance: Taxpayer Funds Spent on Equipment That Was Never Shipped to Yemen." Government Accountability Office. July 2015. 10. <http://www.gao.gov/assets/680/671412.pdf>.
[75] Johnson, Charles Michael. "Security Assistance: Taxpayer Funds Spent on Equipment That Was Never Shipped to Yemen." Government Accountability Office. July 2015. 13-15. <http://www.gao.gov/assets/680/671412.pdf>.
[76] Johnson, Charles Michael. "Security Assistance: Taxpayer Funds Spent on Equipment That Was Never Shipped to Yemen." Government Accountability Office. July 2015. 13-15. <http://www.gao.gov/assets/680/671412.pdf>.
[77] Johnson, Charles Michael. "Security Assistance: Taxpayer Funds Spent on Equipment That Was Never Shipped to Yemen." Government Accountability Office. July 2015. 24. <http://www.gao.gov/assets/680/671412.pdf>.
[78] "Obamacare's Embarrassing and Costly State Exchange Flops." Senate Republican Policy Committee. 15 May 2014. <http://www.rpc.senate.gov/policy-papers/obamacares-embarrassing-and-costly-state-exchange-flops>.
[79] Suderman, Peter. "Obamacare's Failed State Exchanges." *Reason*. 27 Feb. 2014. <https://reason.com/archives/2014/02/27/obamacares-failed-state-exchanges/>.
[80] Mach, Annie and C. Stephen Redhead. "Federal Funding for Health Insurance Exchanges." Congressional Research Service. 29 October 2014. 5. <http://www.lankford.senate.gov/imo/media/doc/Federal%20Funding%20for%20Health%20Insurance%20Exchanges.pdf>.
[81] Mach, Annie and C. Stephen Redhead. "Federal Funding for Health Insurance Exchanges." Congressional Research Service. 29 October 2014. 5. <http://www.lankford.senate.gov/imo/media/doc/Federal%20Funding%20for%20Health%20Insurance%20Exchanges.pdf>.
[82] Levenson, Michael. "Facing 50,000-application Backlog." *Boston Globe*. 13 Feb. 2014. <http://www.bostonglobe.com/metro/2014/02/13/facing-application-backlog-insurance-marketplace-chief-breaks-down-tears/7kvMWfZMczLqsNKQOTE69I/story.html>.
[83] Barry, Dave. "Dave Barry's Review of 2013, the Year of the Zombies." *The Washington Post*. 27 Dec. 2013. <https://www.washingtonpost.com/lifestyle/magazine/dave-barrys-review-of-2013-the-year-of-the-zombies/2013/12/20/c7cfa5fe-5dc2-11e3-bc56-c6ca94801fac_story.html>.
[84] Melvin, Valerie. "State Health Insurance Marketplaces: CMS Should Improve Oversight of State Information Technology Projects." Government Accountability Office. 16 Aug. 2015. PDF 2. <http://www.gao.gov/products/GAO-15-527>.
[85] Bagdoyan, Seto. "Patient Protection and Affordable Care Act: Preliminary Results of Undercover Testing of Enrollment Controls for Health Care Coverage and Consumer Subsidies Provided Under the Act." Government Accountability Office. 23 July 2014. 6. <http://www.gao.gov/products/GAO-14-705T>.
[86] "RI: Medium: Robotic Assistance with Dressing Using Simulation-Based Optimization." National Science Foundation. 8 July 2015. <http://www.nsf.gov/awardsearch/showAward?AWD_ID=1514258&HistoricalAwards=false>.
[87] 17 CFR Chapter II. <https://www.law.cornell.edu/cfr/text/17/chapter-II>.
[88] Raghavan, Sudarsan. "How a Well-intentioned U.S. Law Left Congolese Miners Jobless." *The Washington Post*. 30 Nov. 2014. <https://www.washingtonpost.com/world/africa/how-a-well-intentioned-us-law-left-congolese-miners-jobless/2014/11/30/14b5924e-69d3-11e4-9fb4-a622dae742a2_story.html>.
[89] Gianopoulos, Kimberly. "Conflict Minerals: Stakeholder Options for Responsible Sourcing Are Expanding, but More Information on Smelters Is Needed." Government Accountability Office. May 2014. PDF 2. <http://www.gao.gov/assets/670/664440.pdf>.
[90] "National Highway System Questions & Answers." Federal Highway Administration. 23 May 2013. <http://www.fhwa.dot.gov/map21/qandas/qanhs.cfm>.
[91] "National Highway System Questions & Answers." Federal Highway Administration. 23 May 2013. <http://www.fhwa.dot.gov/map21/qandas/qanhs.cfm>.
[92] Brown, Eliot. "Ads, Not Tenants, Make Times Square." *Wall Street Journal*. 25 Dec. 2012. <http://www.wsj.com/articles/SB10001424127887323476304578199310470733342?alg=y>.
[93] "The Wild and Free-Roaming Horses and Burros Act of 1971." Bureau of Land Management. <http://www.blm.gov/or/regulations/files/whbact_1971.pdf>.

[94] "History and Facts." Bureau of Land Management. 24 Aug. 2015. <http://www.blm.gov/wo/st/en/prog/whbprogram/history_and_facts.html>.
[95] "Quick Facts." Bureau of Land Management. 30 Oct. 2015. < http://www.blm.gov/wo/st/en/prog/whbprogram/history_and_facts/quick_facts.html>.
[96] "Investigative Report of Bureau of Land Management Wild Horse Buyer." U.S Department of the Interior – Office of the Inspector General. 23 Oct. 2015. <https://www.doioig.gov/sites/doioig.gov/files/WildHorseBuyer_Public.pdf>.
[97] *Congressional briefing from BLM on June 30, 2015.*
[98] A Google search for "political polarization" and "media" turned up about 138,000 hits, including 11,800 scholarly journals.
[99] "Collaborative Research: A New Design for Identifying Persuasion Effects and Selection in Media Exposure Experiments via Patient Preference Trials." National Science Foundation. 10 Aug. 2015. <http://www.nsf.gov/awardsearch/showAward?AWD_ID=1528487>.
[100] "NSF at a Glance." National Science Foundation. <http://www.nsf.gov/about/glance.jsp>.
[101] "NSF's Merit Review Process." National Science Foundation. <http://www.nsf.gov/news/mmg/mmg_disp.jsp?med_id=76467>.
[102] "I-Corps: Practical and Provably Secure Random Number Generator."National Science Foundation. 17 Nov. 2014. <http://www.nsf.gov/awardsearch/showAward?AWD_ID=1464476>.
[103] "I-Corps: Practical and Provably Secure Random Number Generator."National Science Foundation. 17 Nov. 2014. <http://www.nsf.gov/awardsearch/showAward?AWD_ID=1464476>.
[104] Sopko, John. "$36 Million Command and Control Facility at Camp Leatherneck, Afghanistan: Unwatned, Unneeded, and Unused." Special Inspector General for Afghanistan Reconstruction. May 2015. <https://www.sigar.mil/pdf/special%20projects/SIGAR-15-57-SP.pdf>.
[105] "ABB Impacts Assessment for Project Review – March 6, 2014." Fish and Wildlife Service – Oklahoma Ecological Services Field Office. 6 Mar. 2014. 1. <http://www.fws.gov/southwest/es/oklahoma/documents/abb/abb%20impact%20assessment%20for%20project%20reviews_6mar2014.pdf>.
[106] Storer, Fred. "Engineering firm asks Interior Secretary Jewell to address policies of the US Fish and Wildlife Serviceregarding the endangered American Burying Beetle." Osages You Need to Know. 3 June 2015. 1. < http://www.osages-you-need-to-know.com/upload/2015-06-03%20American%20Burying%20Beetle.pdf>.
[107] "FY 2016 Federal Funding for Programs Serving Tribes and Native American Communities." Department of Interior. 2015. 1-4. <https://www.doi.gov/sites/doi.gov/files/migrated/budget/upload/FY2016NativeAmericanCrosscut.pdf>.
[108] "Indian Affairs: Budget Justifications and Performance Information- Fiscal Year 2016." Department of the Interior. 2015. IA-ST-2. <https://www.doi.gov/sites/doi.gov/files/migrated/budget/appropriations/2016/upload/FY2016_IA_Greenbook.pdf>.
[109] "Schools." Bureau of Indian Education. <http://www.bie.edu/Schools/index.htm>.
[110] "Johnson- O'Malley." Bureau of Indian Education. <http://www.bie.edu/JOM/>.
[111] "Fiscal Year 2016 Budget Request." Department of Education. 2015. <http://www2.ed.gov/about/overview/budget/budget16/justifications/f-indianed.pdf >.
[112] "Indian Affairs: Budget Justifications and Performance Information- Fiscal Year 2016." Department of Interior. 2015. IA-BIE-7. <https://www.doi.gov/sites/doi.gov/files/migrated/budget/appropriations/2016/upload/FY2016_IA_Greenbook.pdf>.
[113] "2015 Native American Language Preservation and Maintenance Grant Awards." Administration for Native Americans. (2015). <http://www.acf.hhs.gov/programs/ana/news/2015-native-american-language-preservation-grants>.
[114] Emrey-Arras, Melissa. "Bureau of Indian Education Needs to Improve Oversight of School Spending." Government Accountability Office. Nov. 2014. 13. <http://www.gao.gov/assets/670/666890.pdf>.
[115] Emrey-Arras, Melissa. "Bureau of Indian Education Needs to Improve Oversight of School Spending." Government Accountability Office. Nov. 2014. 21. <http://www.gao.gov/assets/670/666890.pdf>.
[116] Emrey-Arras, Melissa. "Further Actions on GAO Recommendations Needed to Address Systemic Management Challenges with Indian Education." Government Accountability Office. 13 May 2015. 18. <http://www.gao.gov/assets/680/670192.pdf>.
[117] "Congressional Justifications." Department of Housing and Urban Development. 2015. <http://portal.hud.gov/hudportal/documents/huddoc?id=FY16-CJE-EntireFile.pdf>.
[118] "Congressional Justifications." Department of Housing and Urban Development. 2015. <http://portal.hud.gov/hudportal/documents/huddoc?id=FY16-CJE-EntireFile.pdf>.

[119] "Budget Justifications and Performance Information Fiscal Year 2016 – Indian Affairs." Department of the Interior. 2015. IA-ST-1. <https://www.doi.gov/sites/doi.gov/files/migrated/budget/appropriations/2016/upload/FY2016_IA_Greenbook.pdf>.
[120] "FY2016 DOJ Request State, Local, and Tribal Law Enforcement Assistance." Department of Justice. 2015. 3. <http://www.justice.gov/sites/default/files/jmd/pages/attachments/2015/01/30/3_2016_state_and_local_chart.pdf>.
[121] "FY2016 DOJ Request State, Local, and Tribal Law Enforcement Assistance." Department of Justice. 2015. 3. <http://www.justice.gov/sites/default/files/jmd/pages/attachments/2015/01/30/3_2016_state_and_local_chart.pdf>.
[122] "Congressional Justifications." Department of Housing and Urban Development. 2015. 11-4. <http://portal.hud.gov/hudportal/documents/huddoc?id=FY16-CJE-EntireFile.pdf>.
[123] "Indian Affairs: Budget Justifications and Performance Information- Fiscal Year 2016." Department of the Interior. 2015. IA-ST-2. <https://www.doi.gov/sites/doi.gov/files/migrated/budget/appropriations/2016/upload/FY2016_IA_Greenbook.pdf>.
[124] "Indian Affairs: Budget Justifications and Performance Information- Fiscal Year 2016." Department of the Interior. 2015. IA-ST-2. <https://www.doi.gov/sites/doi.gov/files/migrated/budget/appropriations/2016/upload/FY2016_IA_Greenbook.pdf>.
[125] "Indian Energy Development: Poor Management by BIA Has Hindered Energy Development on Indian Lands." Government Accountability Office. June 2015. 2. <http://www.gao.gov/assets/680/670701.pdf>.
[126] "Indian Energy Development: Poor Management by BIA Has Hindered Energy Development on Indian Lands." Government Accountability Office. June 2015. <http://www.gao.gov/assets/680/670701.pdf>.
[127] "Indian Energy Development: Poor Management by BIA Has Hindered Energy Development on Indian Lands." Government Accountability Office. June 2015. 15. <http://www.gao.gov/assets/680/670701.pdf>.
[128] "Indian Energy Development: Poor Management by BIA Has Hindered Energy Development on Indian Lands." Government Accountability Office. June 2015. 17. <http://www.gao.gov/assets/680/670701.pdf>.
[129] "Indian Energy Development: Poor Management by BIA Has Hindered Energy Development on Indian Lands." Government Accountability Office. June 2015. 21-22. <http://www.gao.gov/assets/680/670701.pdf>.
[130] "Indian Energy Development: Poor Management by BIA Has Hindered Energy Development on Indian Lands." Government Accountability Office. June 2015. 18. <http://www.gao.gov/assets/680/670701.pdf>.
[131] "FY 2016 Department of Labor Budget in Brief." Department of Labor. 2015. 10. <http://www.dol.gov/dol/budget/2016/PDF/FY2016BIB.pdf>.
[132] "Indian Affairs: Budget Justifications and Performance Information- Fiscal Year 2016." Department of the Interior. 2015. IA-ST-1. <https://www.doi.gov/sites/doi.gov/files/migrated/budget/appropriations/2016/upload/FY2016_IA_Greenbook.pdf>.
[133] "Indian Affairs: Budget Justifications and Performance Information- Fiscal Year 2016." Department of the Interior. 2015. IA-ST-1. <https://www.doi.gov/sites/doi.gov/files/migrated/budget/appropriations/2016/upload/FY2016_IA_Greenbook.pdf>.
[134] "FHWA FY 2016 BUDGET." Department of Transportation. 2015. III-3. <https://www.transportation.gov/sites/dot.gov/files/docs/FY2016-BudgetEstimate-FHWA.pdf>.
[135] "Development and Testing LIDAR to Study Insect Responses to Light and Noise." National Parks Service. 11 Sept. 2015. <http://www.grants.gov/web/grants/view-opportunity.html?oppId=278931>.
[136] Kirk, Robert S., and William J. Mallett. "Surface Transportation Program Reauthorization Issues for Congress." Congressional Research Service. 11 Sept. 2015. 4. <http://www.lankford.senate.gov/imo/media/doc/Surface%20Transportation%20Program%20Reauthorization%20Issues%20for%20Congress.pdf>.
[137] "Transportation Alternatives Program (TAP)." Department of Transportation. 10 Oct. 2015. 4. <http://www.fhwa.dot.gov/environment/transportation_alternatives/>.
[138] Kirk, Robert S., and William J. Mallett. "Surface Transportation Program Reauthorization Issues for Congress." Congressional Research Service. 11 Sept. 2015. 8. <http://www.lankford.senate.gov/imo/media/doc/Surface%20Transportation%20Program%20Reauthorization%20Issues%20for%20Congress.pdf>.
[139] "Construction Continues in the I-40 Crosstown Corridor." Oklahoma Department of Transportation. 21 July 2015. <http://www.ok.gov/odot/What's_New/I-40Crosstown.html>.
[140] Lowry, Sean. "The Federal Excise Tax on Motor Fuels and the Highway Trust Fund: Current Law and Legislative History." Congressional Research Services. 23 Feb. 2015. PDF 2. <http://www.lankford.senate.gov/imo/media/doc/The%20Federal%20Excise%20Tax%20on%20Motor%20Fuels%20and%20the%20Highway%20Trust%20Fund%20Current%20Law%20and%20Legislative%20History.pdf>.

[141] McMinimy, Mark and Kelsi Bracmort. "Renewable Fuel Standard (RFS): Overview and Issues." Congressional Research Service. 22 Nov. 2013. 22. <http://www.lankford.senate.gov/imo/media/doc/1st%20Renewable%20Fuel%20Standard%20Overview%20and%20Issues.pdf>.

[142] Bracmort, Kelsi. "The Renewable Fuel Standard (RFS): Cellulosic Biofuels." Congressional Research Service. 31 Aug. 2015. PDF 2. <http://www.lankford.senate.gov/imo/media/doc/The%20Renewable%20Fuel%20Standard%20Cellulosic%20Biofuels.pdf>.

[143] Wyden, Ron. "Provisions in the Chairman's Mark: Expiring Provisions Improvement Reform and Efficiency (EXPIRE) Act." Senate Committee on Finance. 1 April 2014. <http://www.finance.senate.gov/newsroom/chairman/download/?id=e4f905e4-b677-44c0-8f0c-36c1ffdc459f>.

[144] "Summary of Executive Order 12866 – Regulatory Planning and Review." 16 Nov. 2015. <http://www2.epa.gov/laws-regulations/summary-executive-order-12866-regulatory-planning-and-review>.

[145] "Regulatory Planning and Review – Executive Order 12866 of September 30, 1993." Federal Register. 4 Oct. 1993. <https://www.archives.gov/federal-register/executive-orders/pdf/12866.pdf>. "Improving Regulation and Regulatory Review." Federal Register. 21 Jan. 2011. 1-2. <http://www.gpo.gov/fdsys/pkg/FR-2011-01-21/pdf/2011-1385.pdf>.

[146] Graham, John D. "Testimony of John D. Graham: Examining Federal Rulemaking Challenges and Areas of Improvement Within the Existing Regulatory Process," Committee on Homeland Security and Governmental Affairs Subcommittee on Regulatory Affairs and Federal Management Hearing. 19 Mar. 2015. 7. <http://www.hsgac.senate.gov/download/?id=11DF5A77-C9AE-40F0-9D89-3FD79C60BE28>.

[147] Portman, Rob. "S.280 Federal Permitting Improvement Act of 2015." Introduced 28 Jan. 2015. <https://www.congress.gov/bill/114th-congress/senate-bill/280?q=%7B%22search%22%3A%5B%22%5C%22s280%5C%22%22%5D%7D&resultIndex=1>.

[148] Sopko, John. "Gorimar Industrial Park: Lack of Electricity and Water Have Left This $7.7 Million U.S.-funded Industrial Park Underutilized by Afghan Businesses." Special Inspector General for Afghanistan Reconstruction. 27 Jan. 2015. 1-2. <https://www.sigar.mil/pdf/inspections/SIGAR-15-30-IP.pdf>.

[149] "Transaction Details." USA Spending. <https://www.usaspending.gov/transparency/Pages/TransactionDetails.aspx?RecordID=426F9C20-0D99-B741-D71E-77FDA5665FFA&AwardID=6669100&AwardType=C>.

[150] Nabors, Robert L. "VA's Solar Panel Project." 20 July 2015. 1-7. <https://hill.house.gov/sites/hill.house.gov/files/wysiwyg_uploaded/2015-07-20%20--%20VA%20response%20to%20Solar%20Panels%20Letter%20%282%29.pdf>.

[151] Nabors, Robert L. "VA's Solar Panel Project." 20 July 2015. 1-7. <https://hill.house.gov/sites/hill.house.gov/files/wysiwyg_uploaded/2015-07-20%20--%20VA%20response%20to%20Solar%20Panels%20Letter%20%282%29.pdf>.

[152] "Breast Cancer- for Patients." National Cancer Institute. <http://www.cancer.gov/types see: breast cancer>

[153] "DOD Breast Cancer Breakthrough Award Levels 1 and 2." Department of Defense. 25 Aug. 2015. <http://www.grants.gov/web/grants/view-opportunity.html?oppId=278653>.

[154] "DOD Breast Cancer Breakthrough Award Levels 1 and 2." Department of Defense. 25 Aug. 2015. <http://www.grants.gov/web/grants/view-opportunity.html?oppId=278653>.

[155] "Lifeline Program for Low-Income Consumers." Federal Communications Commission. 6 Nov. 2015. <https://www.fcc.gov/lifeline>.

[156] "Moving Forward: 2014 Annual Report." Universal Service Administrative Company. 2014. 9. <http://www.usac.org/_res/documents/about/pdf/annual-reports/usac-annual-report-2014.pdf>.

[157] "Lifeline: Promoting Telephone Subscribership on Tribal Lands." Federal Communications Commission. 28 Aug. 2015. <https://www.fcc.gov/guides/promoting-telephone-subscribership-tribal-lands-0>.

[158] "LI08 Lifeline Subscribers by State or Jurisdiction January 2015 through June 2015." Universal Service Administrative Company. 2015. <https://www.usac.org/about/tools/fcc/filings/2015/Q4/LI08%20Lifeline%20Subscribers%20by%20State%20or%20Jurisdiction%20-%20January%202015%20through%20June%202015.xlsx>. *For dollar amount, see page one:* <https://apps.fcc.gov/edocs_public/attachmatch/DOC-333992A5.pdf>.

[159] Pai, Ajit. "Dissenting Statement of Commissioner Ajit Pai." Federal Communications Commission. 2015. 2. <https://apps.fcc.gov/edocs_public/attachmatch/DOC-333992A5.pdf>.

[160] "LI08 Lifeline Subscribers by State or Jurisdiction January 2015 through June 2015." Universal Service Administrative Company. 2015.

<https://www.usac.org/about/tools/fcc/filings/2015/Q4/LI08%20Lifeline%20Subscribers%20by%20State%20or%20Jurisdiction%20-%20January%202015%20through%20June%202015.xlsx>.

[161] "Second Further Notice of Proposed Rulemaking, Order on Reconsideration, Second Report and Order, and Memorandum Opinion and Order." Federal Communications Commission. 22 June 2015. 87. <http://transition.fcc.gov/Daily_Releases/Daily_Business/2015/db0622/FCC-15-71A1.pdf>.

[162] Kuriloff, Aaron and Darrell Preston. "In Stadium Building Spree, U.S. Taxpayers Lose $4 Billion." *Bloomberg Business*. 5 Sept. 2012. <http://www.bloomberg.com/news/articles/2012-09-05/in-stadium-building-spree-u-s-taxpayers-lose-4-billion>.

[163] "General Explanations of the Administration's Fiscal Year 2016 Revenue Proposals." Department of the Treasury. Feb. 2015. 293. <http://www.treasury.gov/resource-center/tax-policy/Documents/General-Explanations-FY2016.pdf>.

[164] Kuriloff, Aaron and Darrell Preston. "In Stadium Building Spree, U.S. Taxpayers Lose $4 Billion." *Bloomberg Business*. 5 Sept. 2012. <http://www.bloomberg.com/news/articles/2012-09-05/in-stadium-building-spree-u-s-taxpayers-lose-4-billion>.

[165] "A Review of CBO's Activities in 2014 Under the Unfunded Mandates Reform Act." Congressional Budget Office. Mar. 2015. 40. <https://www.cbo.gov/sites/default/files/114th-congress-2015-2016/reports/50051-UMRA2_1.pdf>.

[166] "National School Lunch Program and School Breakfast Program: Nutrition Standards for All Foods Sold in School as Required by the Healthy, Hunger-Free Kids Act of 2010, Interim Rule." Federal Register. 28 June 2013. <http://www.gpo.gov/fdsys/pkg/FR-2013-06-28/pdf/2013-15249.pdf>.

[167] Fantone, Denise. "Federal Mandates: Few Rules Trigger Unfunded Mandates Reform Act." Government Accountability Office. 15 Feb. 2011. PDF 2. <http://www.gao.gov/assets/130/125488.pdf>.

[168] Foxx, Virginia. "Unfunded Mandates Information & Transparency Act." 18 Nov. 2015. <http://foxx.house.gov/legislation/umita.htm>.

[169] "Multinational Species Conservation Acts." Fish and Wildlife Service. <http://www.fws.gov/international/laws-treaties-agreements/us-conservation-laws/multinational-species-conservation-acts.html>.

[170] Sheikh, Pervaze and M. Lynne Corn. "International Species Conservation Funds." Congressional Research Service. 17 Dec 2013. 1. <http://www.lankford.senate.gov/imo/media/doc/International%20Species%20Conservation%20Funds.pdf>.

[171] Sheikh, Pervaze and M. Lynne Corn. "International Species Conservation Funds." Congressional Research Service. 17 Dec 2013. 1. <http://www.lankford.senate.gov/imo/media/doc/International%20Species%20Conservation%20Funds.pdf>.

[172] Hillman, Richard. "Security: Overlapping Disability and Unemployment Benefits Should Be Evaluated for Potential Savings." Government Accountability Office. 31 July 2012. PDF 2. <http://www.gao.gov/assets/600/593203.pdf>.

[173] Hillman, Richard. "Security: Overlapping Disability and Unemployment Benefits Should Be Evaluated for Potential Savings." Government Accountability Office. 31 July 2012. PDF 2. <http://www.gao.gov/assets/600/593203.pdf>.

[174] Morton, William. "Concurrent Receipt of Social Security Disability Insurance (SSDI) and Unemployment Insurance (UI): Background and Legislative Proposals." Congressional Research Service. 31 July 2015. 17. <https://www.fas.org/sgp/crs/misc/R43471.pdf>.

[175] "Social Security Disability Insurance and Unemployment Benefits Double Dip Elimination Act of 2015 (H.R. 918)." Committee on Ways and Means. 12 Feb. 2015. <http://waysandmeans.house.gov/wp-content/uploads/2015/06/HR-918-Fact-Sheet-Final.pdf>.

[176] Morton, William. "Concurrent Receipt of Social Security Disability Insurance (SSDI) and Unemployment Insurance (UI): Background and Legislative Proposals." Congressional Research Service. 31 July 2015. 17. <https://www.fas.org/sgp/crs/misc/R43471.pdf>.

[177] "Definition of Navigable Waters of the US." 33 CFR Part 329. <http://www.nap.usace.army.mil/Portals/39/docs/regulatory/regs/33cfr329.pdf>.

[178] "Protection of the Environment – Environmental Protection Agency – Water Programs." Federal Register. 40 C.F.R §110, 112, 116. <http://www.ecfr.gov/cgi-bin/text-idx?SID=07b2d546999e30ed5d116dbda9345d0c&mc=true&tpl=/ecfrbrowse/Title40/40CIsubchapD.tpl>.

[179] Peabody, John W. "Memorandum For Assistant Secretary of the Army for Civil Works." 27 April 2015. Department of the Army. <https://www.dropbox.com/sh/bgdwo03e9rsr1ff/AADYJ40Es5qAnDyLhnKJfQK4a/HOGR%20%231%20FINAL%2020150728%20April%2027%20Peabody%20Memo.pdf?dl=0>.

[180] "So, Farmers Have to Get Permits. What's so Bad About That? American Farm Bureau Federation. <http://ditchtherule.fb.org/custom_page/so-farmers-have-to-get-permits-whats-so-bad-about-that/>.

[181] Barrasso, John. "S. 1140 The Federal Water Quality Protection Act," Introduced 30 Apr. 2015, 10 Nov. 2015, <https://www.congress.gov/bill/114th-congress/senate-bill/1140?q=%7B%22search%22%3A%5B%22%5C%22s1140%5C%22%22%5D%7D&resultIndex=1>.

[182] Ernst, Joni. "S.J.Res.22 – A Joint Resolution Providing for Congressional Disapproval Under Chapter 8 of Title 5, United States Code, of the Rule Submitted by the Corps of Engineers and the Environmental Protection Agency Relating to the Definition of 'Waters of the United States' Under the Federal Water Pollution Control Act." Introduced 17 Sept. 2015, <https://www.congress.gov/bill/114th-congress/senate-joint-resolution/22?q=%7B%22search%22%3A%5B%22%5C%22sjres22%5C%22%22%5D%7D&resultIndex=1>.

[183] "Global Labor Program." Agency for International Development. 24 July 2015. <http://www.grants.gov/web/grants/view-opportunity.html?oppId=278099>.

[184] "Global Labor Program." Agency for International Development. 24 July 2015. <http://www.grants.gov/web/grants/view-opportunity.html?oppId=278099>.

[185] "Global Labor Program." Agency for International Development. 24 July 2015. <http://www.grants.gov/web/grants/view-opportunity.html?oppId=278099>.

[186] "U.S. Spends $250,000 to Make Morocco." Judicial Watch. 15 May 2015. <http://www.judicialwatch.org/blog/2015/05/u-s-spends-250000-to-make-morocco-green/>.

[187] "Morocco." Department of State. <http://www.state.gov/e/oes/eqt/trade/morocco/index.htm>.

[188] "Michigan Brewery Gets Fed Grant for Solar Panel Project." *The Detroit News*. 14 Aug. 2015. <http://www.detroitnews.com/story/business/2015/08/14/mich-brewery-gets-fed-grant-solar-panel-project/31749859/>.

[189] Freeman, Weldon. "USDA Invests $6.7 Million in 544 Renewable Energy and Energy Efficiency Projects Nationwide." Department of Agriculture. 10 June 2015. <http://www.usda.gov/wps/portal/usda/usdamediafb?contentid=2015%2F06%2F0166.xml&printable=true&contentidonly=true>.

[190] Watson, Bart. "U.S. Passes 4,000 Breweries." Brewers Association. 28 Sept. 2015. <https://www.brewersassociation.org/insights/4000-breweries/>.

[191] Watson, Bart. "U.S. Passes 4,000 Breweries." Brewers Association. 28 Sept. 2015. <https://www.brewersassociation.org/insights/4000-breweries/>.

[192] "National Beer Sales & Production Data." Brewers Association. <https://www.brewersassociation.org/statistics/national-beer-sales-production-data/>.

[193] "Defining and Delimiting the Exemptions for Executive, Administrative, Professional, Outside Sales and Computer Employees." Department of Labor. 2015. <http://www.dol.gov/whd/overtime/NPRM2015/OT-NPRM.pdf>.

[194] Watson, Bart. "New Overtime Rule Add Costs to Small Businesses and Hurts Workers." National Federation of Independent Business. 19 Oct. 2015. <http://www.nfib.com/article/new-overtime-rule-add-costs-to-small-businesses-and-hurts-workers-70007/>.

[195] Watson, Bart. "New Overtime Rule Add Costs to Small Businesses and Hurts Workers." National Federation of Independent Business. 19 Oct. 2015. <http://www.nfib.com/article/new-overtime-rule-add-costs-to-small-businesses-and-hurts-workers-70007/>.

[196] Shearman, J. Craig. "One-Size-Fits-All Overtime Proposal Fails to Consider Cost-of-Living." National Retail Federation. 1 Sept. 2015. <https://nrf.com/media/press-releases/one-size-fits-all-overtime-proposal-fails-consider-cost-of-living>.

[197] "Defining and Delimiting the Exemptions for Executive, Administrative, Professional, Outside Sales and Computer Employees." *Federal Register*. 6 July 2015. <https://www.federalregister.gov/articles/2015/07/06/2015-15464/defining-and-delimiting-the-exemptions-for-executive-administrative-professional-outside-sales-and>.

[198] "Defining and Delimiting the Exemptions for Executive, Administrative, Professional, Outside Sales and Computer Employees." Department of Labor. 2015. <http://www.dol.gov/whd/overtime/NPRM2015/OT-NPRM.pdf>.

[199] Goldbeck, Dan. ""White Collar" Overtime Expansion." American Action Forum. 13 July 2015. <http://americanactionforum.org/regulation-review/white-collar-overtime-expansion>.

[200] Tang, Rachel Y. "Essential Air Service." Congressional Research Service. 3 Sept. 2015. PDF 2. <http://www.lankford.senate.gov/imo/media/doc/Essential%20Air%20Service.pdf>.

[201] Tang, Rachel Y. "Essential Air Service." Congressional Research Service. 3 Sept. 2015. 6. <http://www.lankford.senate.gov/imo/media/doc/Essential%20Air%20Service.pdf>.

[202] "Is Essential Air Service Wasting Taxpayer Money?" *CBS News*. 24 Feb. 2015. <http://www.cbsnews.com/news/government-subsidized-essential-air-service-waste-of-taxpayer-money-some-say/>.

[203] "Is Essential Air Service Wasting Taxpayer Money?" *CBS News*. 24 Feb. 2015. <http://www.cbsnews.com/news/government-subsidized-essential-air-service-waste-of-taxpayer-money-some-say/>.

[204] "EAS Communities in the 48 Contiguous States Located within 210 Miles from the Nearest Large or Medium Hub Subject to the $200 per Passenger Subsidy Cap." Department of Transportation. Sept. 2015. 1-4. <https://www.transportation.gov/sites/dot.gov/files/docs/Status%20report-%24200%20compliance-Sep2015.pdf>.

[205] Oberholtz, Chris. "Investigation Finds Taxpayers Fund Nearly Empty Flights." *KCTV5*. 24 Feb. 2015. <http://www.kctv5.com/story/28189761/investigation-finds-taxpayers-fund-nearly-empty-flights>.

[206] Dillingham, Gerald. "Status of Air Service to Small Communities and the Federal Programs Involved." Government Accountability Office. 30 Apr. 2014. PDF 2. <http://www.gao.gov/products/GAO-14-454T>.

[207] "Eliminate the Essential Air Service Program." Congressional Budget Office. 06 Aug. 2009. <https://www.cbo.gov/budget-options/2014/49724>.

[208] "The FPS Vehicle Fleet Is Not Managed Effectively." Department of Homeland Security. 21 Sept. 2015. 4. <https://www.oig.dhs.gov/assets/Mgmt/2016/OIG-16-02-Oct15.pdf>.

[209] "The FPS Vehicle Fleet Is Not Managed Effectively." Department of Homeland Security. 21 Sept. 2015. 2. <https://www.oig.dhs.gov/assets/Mgmt/2016/OIG-16-02-Oct15.pdf>.

[210] "The FPS Vehicle Fleet Is Not Managed Effectively." Department of Homeland Security. 21 Sept. 2015. 3. <https://www.oig.dhs.gov/assets/Mgmt/2016/OIG-16-02-Oct15.pdf>.

[211] "The FPS Vehicle Fleet Is Not Managed Effectively." Department of Homeland Security. 21 Sept. 2015. 4. <https://www.oig.dhs.gov/assets/Mgmt/2016/OIG-16-02-Oct15.pdf>.

[212] "Motor Vehicle Management Overview," General Service Administration. <http://www.gsa.gov/portal/content/104602> *see "FY2014 Federal Fleet Report."*

[213] Fleming, Susan. "Overall Increase in Number of Vehicles Masks That Some Agencies Decreased Their Fleets." Government Accountability Office. 2 Aug. 2012. PDF 2. <http://www.gao.gov/assets/600/593249.pdf>.

[214] "Motor Vehicle Management Overview," General Service Administration. <http://www.gsa.gov/portal/content/104602> *see "FY2014 Federal Fleet Report."*

[215] Shaheen, Jeanne. "S. 427 – Drive Lesse Act." Introduced: 10 Feb. 2015. <https://www.congress.gov/bill/114th-congress/senate-bill/427>.

[216] Bravin, Jess. "Supreme Court Strikes Down New Deal-Era Raisin Price-Support Program." *The Wall Street Journal*. 22 June 2015. <http://www.wsj.com/articles/supreme-court-strikes-down-new-deal-era-raisin-price-support-program-1434986839>.

[217] "Market Access Program (MAP)." Department of Agriculture. <http://www.fas.usda.gov/programs/market-access-program-map>.

[218] *To browse the 5 programs, visit:* http://www.fas.usda.gov/programs/search?f[0]=field_topics%3A53

[219] "MAP Funding Allocations - FY 2015." Department of Agriculture. <http://www.fas.usda.gov/programs/market-access-program-map/map-funding-allocations-fy-2015>.

[220] "What's Being Harvested Now?" Fresno County Farm Bureau. <http://www.fcfb.org/News/HarvestTime-Seasons/HarvestTime-All.php>.

[221] *Marvin D. Horne, et. al., v. Department of Agriculture.* 22 June 2015. <http://www.supremecourt.gov/opinions/14pdf/14-275_c0n2.pdf>.

[222] Bravin, Jess. "Supreme Court Strikes Down New Deal-Era Raisin Price-Support Program." *The Wall Street Journal*. 22 June 2015. <http://www.wsj.com/articles/supreme-court-strikes-down-new-deal-era-raisin-price-support-program-1434986839>.

[223] "Testimony of Thomas A. Schatz President, Citizens Against Government Waste." Senate Committee on Homeland Security and Government Affairs Subcommittee on Federal Spending Oversight and Emergency Management. 10 June 2015. 17. <http://www.idfa.org/docs/default-source/d-news/final-testimony-of-thomas-a-schatz__president-citizens-against-government-waste__senate-hsgac__6-10-2015.pdf?sfvrsn=2>.

[224] "Tax Expenditures Compendium of Background Material on Individual Provisions." Congressional Research Service. Dec. 2014. 22. < http://www.gpo.gov/fdsys/pkg/CPRT-113SPRT91950/pdf/CPRT-113SPRT91950.pdf>.

[225] "Provisions in the Chairman's Mark: Expiring Provisions Improvement Reform and Efficiency (EXPIRE) Act." Senate Committee on Finance. 21 May 2014. 8. <http://www.finance.senate.gov/legislation/download/?id=c653c7b4-8731-4b31-a2eb-2cce5114ece8>.

[226] "Regulating Coal Mines." Department of Interior. 21 May 2015. <http://www.osmre.gov/programs/rcm.shtm>.

[227] "Grant Awards Announced for 2015." Blue Ridge National Heritage Area. 10 Feb. 2015. <http://www.blueridgeheritage.com/heritage/2015-grant-awards>.

[228] "About the Blue Ridge National Heritage Area." Blue Ridge National Heritage Area. <http://www.blueridgeheritage.com/about>.

[229] DeNavas-Walt, Carmen and Bernadette Proctor. "Income and Poverty in the United States: 2014." Census Bureau. Sept. 2015. 6. <http://www.census.gov/content/dam/Census/library/publications/2015/demo/p60-252.pdf>.

[230] Dicken, John. "Prescription Drugs: Comparison of DOD and VA Direct Purchase Prices." Government Accountability Office. April 2013. 9. <http://www.gao.gov/assets/660/654019.pdf>.
[231] Dicken, John. "Prescription Drugs: Comparison of DOD, Medicaid, and Medicare Part D Retail Reimbursement Prices." Government Accountability Office. June 2014. PDF 2. <http://www.gao.gov/products/GAO-14-578>.
[232] "Office of Public and Indian Housing, Washington, DC Overincome Families Residing in Public Housing Units," Department of Housing and Urban Development. 21 July 2015. PDF 3. <https://www.hudoig.gov/sites/default/files/documents/2015-PH-0002.pdf>.
[233] Needham, Vicki. "HUD audit finds 25,000 ineligible families in public housing," *The Hill*, 17 Aug. 2015. <http://thehill.com/policy/finance/251330-hud-audit-finds-25000-ineligible-families-in-public-housing>.
[234] Needham, Vicki. "HUD audit finds 25,000 ineligible families in public housing," *The Hill*, 17 Aug. 2015. <http://thehill.com/policy/finance/251330-hud-audit-finds-25000-ineligible-families-in-public-housing>.
[235] Rein, Lisa. "Congressman threatens to strip HUD of $104 million because of public housing tenants who make too much," *The Washington Post*, 12 Oct. 2015. <https://www.washingtonpost.com/news/federal-eye/wp/2015/10/12/fla-congressman-says-hell-strip-hud-of-104-million-unless-it-clarifies-policy-on-public-housing-tenants-who-make-too-much/>.
[236] Onishi, Norimitsu. "Empty Ebola Clinics in Liberia Are Seen as Misstep in U.S. Relief Effort." *New York Times*. 11 April 2015. <http://www.nytimes.com/2015/04/12/world/africa/idle-ebola-clinics-in-liberia-are-seen-as-misstep-in-us-relief-effort.html>.
[237] Onishi, Norimitsu. "Empty Ebola Clinics in Liberia Are Seen as Misstep in U.S. Relief Effort." *New York Times*. 11 April 2015. <http://www.nytimes.com/2015/04/12/world/africa/idle-ebola-clinics-in-liberia-are-seen-as-misstep-in-us-relief-effort.html>.
[238] Sieff, Kevin. "U.S.-built Ebola Treatment Centers in Liberia are Nearly Empty as Outbreak Fades." *Washington Post*. 18 January 2015. <https://www.washingtonpost.com/world/africa/us-built-ebola-treatment-centers-in-liberia-are-nearly-empty-as-disease-fades/2015/01/18/9acc3e2c-9b52-11e4-86a3-1b56f64925f6_story.html>.
[239] *Quarterly update provided by the Department of State to the Senate Appropriations Committee.*
[240] *Quarterly update provided by the Department of Health and Human Services to the Senate Appropriations Committee.*
[241] "Ebola Situation Report." World Health Organization. 11 November 2015. <http://apps.who.int/ebola/current-situation/ebola-situation-report-11-november-2015>.
[242] "About SIGAR." Special Inspector General for Afganistan Reconstruction. <https://www.sigar.mil/about/index.aspx?SSR=1&SubSSR=1&WP=About%20SIGAR>.
[243] Sopko, John. "Tarakhil Power Plant in Kabul, Afghanistan." Letter to Donald "Larry" Sampler. 7 Aug. 2015. <https://www.sigar.mil/pdf/special%20projects/SIGAR-15-80-SP.pdf>.
[244] Sopko, John. "Tarakhil Power Plant in Kabul, Afghanistan." Letter to Donald "Larry" Sampler. 7 Aug. 2015. <https://www.sigar.mil/pdf/special%20projects/SIGAR-15-80-SP.pdf>.
[245] Asa, Randall. "Review of Sustainability of Operations at Afghanistan's Tarakhil Power Plant." Office of Inspector General – U.S. Agency for International Development. 19 June 2014. 6. <http://pdf.usaid.gov/pdf_docs/pbaaa531.pdf>.
[246] "Understanding the Mechanisms for Disengagement from Contentious Political Interaction." National Science Foundation. 4 September 2014. <http://www.nsf.gov/awardsearch/showAward?AWD_ID=1423788>.
[247] "Understanding the Mechanisms for Disengagement from Contentious Political Interaction." National Science Foundation. 4 September 2014. <http://www.nsf.gov/awardsearch/showAward?AWD_ID=1423788>.
[248] "About the National Science Foundation." National Science Foundation. <http://www.nsf.gov/about/>.
[249] NPR, Robert Wood Johnson Foundation, Harvard School of Public Health. "The Burden of Stress in America." 2014. <http://www.rwjf.org/content/dam/farm/reports/surveys_and_polls/2014/rwjf414295/subassets/rwjf414295_1>.
[250] Ingraham, Christopher. "Politicians are the No. 1 Cause of Daily Stress in Our Lives." *The Washington Post*. 10 July 2014. <https://www.washingtonpost.com/news/wonk/wp/2014/07/10/politicians-are-the-no-1-cause-of-daily-stress-in-our-lives/>.
[251] Office of Justice Programs. "About the Office for Victims of Crime." <http://www.ovc.gov/about/victimsfund.html>.
[252] Office of Justice Programs. "About the Office for Victims of Crime." <http://www.ovc.gov/about/victimsfund.html>
[253] Office of Justice Programs. "About the Office for Victims of Crime." <http://www.ovc.gov/about/victimsfund.html>.
[254] Sessions, Jeff. "Sessions Outlines Spending Increases and Gimmicks in Appropriations Package." 31 Oct. 2011. <http://www.sessions.senate.gov/public/index.cfm/2011/10/sessions-outlines-spending-increases-and-gimmicks-in-appropriations-package>.
[255] "Understanding Age-Related Changes in Relationship Maintenance Strategies." The National Science Foundation. 10 February 2015. <http://www.nsf.gov/awardsearch/showAward?AWD_ID=1451492&HistoricalAwards=false>.
[256] "Understanding Age-Related Changes in Relationship Maintenance Strategies." The National Science Foundation. 10 Feburary 2015. <http://www.nsf.gov/awardsearch/showAward?AWD_ID=1451492&HistoricalAwards=false>.

[257] "Regulatory Guidance Processes: Selected Departments Could Strengthen Internal Control and Dissemination Practices." U.S. Government Accountability Office. Apr. 2015. 30. <http://www.gao.gov/assets/670/669688.pdf>.

[258] "OFCCP Guidance Documents," U.S. Department of Labor Office of Federal Contract Compliance Programs (OFCCP). <http://www.dol.gov/ofccp/TAguides/OFCCP_SGD_Information.htm>.

[259] "Carbon Pollution Emission Guidelines for Existing Stationary Sources: Electric Utility Generating Units; Final Rule." Federal Register. 23 Oct. 2015. <http://www.gpo.gov/fdsys/pkg/FR-2015-10-23/pdf/2015-22842.pdf>.

[260] "Proposed Clean Power Plan would Accelerate Renewable Additions and Coal Plant Retirements." Energy Information Administration. 5 June 2015. <http://www.eia.gov/todayinenergy/detail.cfm?id=21532>.

[261] Weber, Harry. "Clean Power Plan to Shutter 4,000 MW of Texas Coal Output," *Bloomberg Business.* 16 Oct. 2015. <http://www.bloomberg.com/news/articles/2015-10-16/texas-says-clean-power-plan-to-shutter-4-000-mw-of-coal-output>.

[262] Tribe, Laurence E. "The Clean Power Plan Is Unconstitutional." *The Wall Street Journal.* 22 Dec. 2014. <http://www.wsj.com/articles/laurence-tribe-the-epas-clean-power-plan-is-unconstitutional-1419293203>.

[263] McConnell, Mitch. "S.J.Res.23- A joint resolution providing for congressional disapproval under chapter 8 of title 5, United States Code, of a rule submitted by the Environmental Protection Agency relating to "Standards of Performance for Greenhouse Gas Emissions from New, Modified, and Reconstructed Stationary Sources: Electric Utility Generating Units." Introduced: 26 Oct. 2015. <https://www.congress.gov/bill/114th-congress/senate-joint-resolution/23/text>. & Capito, Shelley Moore. "S.J.Res.24 - A joint resolution providing for congressional disapproval under chapter 8 of title 5, United States Code, of a rule submitted by the Environmental Protection Agency relating to "Carbon Pollution Emission Guidelines for Existing Stationary Sources: Electric Utility Generating Units." Introduced 26. Oct. 2015. <https://www.congress.gov/bill/114th-congress/senate-joint-resolution/24/text>.

[264] "U.S. Ambassadors Fund for Cultural Preservation, *Awards List.*" Department of State. 2014. 1. <http://eca.state.gov/files/bureau/afcp2014_awards_list.pdf>.

[265] "U.S. Ambassadors Fund for Cultural Preservation, *Awards List.*" Department of State. 2014. 2. <http://eca.state.gov/files/bureau/afcp2014_awards_list.pdf>.

[266] "U.S. Ambassadors Fund for Cultural Preservation, *Awards List.*" Department of State. 2014. 2. <http://eca.state.gov/files/bureau/afcp2014_awards_list.pdf>.

[267] "The U.S. Ambassadors Fund for Cultural Preservation – Annual Report." Department of State. 2011. 61. <http://eca.state.gov/files/bureau/afcp_2010_annual_report.pdf>.

[268] "The U.S. Ambassador's Fund for Cultural Preservation – Annual Report." Department of State. 2011. 44. <http://eca.state.gov/files/bureau/afcp_2010_annual_report.pdf>.

[269] "The U.S. Ambassador's Fund for Cultural Preservation – Annual Report." Department of State. 2009. 25. <http://eca.state.gov/files/bureau/afcp2008annual_report_final.pdf>.

[270] "The U.S. Ambassador's Fund for Cultural Preservation – Annual Report." Department of State. 2010. 35. <http://eca.state.gov/files/bureau/afcp_2010_annual_report.pdf >.

[271] "Budget Justification, Fiscal Year 2015." U.S. Department of State. 2015. <http://www.state.gov/documents/organization/222898.pdf>.

[272] "Ambassadors Fund for Cultural Preservation." Department of State. <http://eca.state.gov/cultural-heritage-center/ambassadors-fund-cultural-preservation>.

[273] Alves, Ted. "Food and Beverage Service: Potential Opportunities to Reduce Losses." Amtrak Office of the Inspector General. 31 October 2013. PDF 2. <https://www.amtrakoig.gov/sites/default/files/reports/oig-a-2014-001.pdf>.

[274] Alves, Ted. "Food and Beverage Service: Potential Opportunities to Reduce Losses." Amtrak Office of the Inspector General. 31 October 2013. PDF 3. <https://www.amtrakoig.gov/sites/default/files/reports/oig-a-2014-001.pdf>.

[275] Peterman, David Randall and John Frittelli. "Issues in the Reauthorization of Amtrak."Congressional Research Service. 11 March 2015. 22. <http://www.lankford.senate.gov/imo/media/doc/Issues%20in%20the%20Reauthorization%20of%20Amtrak.pdf>.

[276] "Congressional Budget Justification. Appendix 1." Department of State. 2015. 197. <http://www.state.gov/documents/organization/236393.pdf>.

[277] "Audit Report: Numberholders Age 112 or Older Who Did Not Have a Death Entry on the Numident." Inspector General for Social Security Administration. 2015. 1. <http://oig.ssa.gov/sites/default/files/audit/full/pdf/A-06-14-34030_0.pdf>.

[278] "Audit Report: Numberholders Age 112 or Older Who Did Not Have a Death Entry on the Numident." Inspector General for Social Security Administration. 2015. 1. <http://oig.ssa.gov/sites/default/files/audit/full/pdf/A-06-14-34030_0.pdf>.

[279] "Audit Report: Numberholders Age 112 or Older Who Did Not Have a Death Entry on the Numident." Inspector General for Social Security Administration. 2015. 8. <http://oig.ssa.gov/sites/default/files/audit/full/pdf/A-06-14-34030_0.pdf>.

[280] Ohlemacher, Stephen. "Report: Social security numbers active for 6.5 million people aged 112." *PBS*. 14 March 2015. <http://www.pbs.org/newshour/rundown/death-stop-social-security-payments/>.

[281] "Audit Report: Numberholders Age 112 or Older Who Did Not Have a Death Entry on the Numident." Inspector General for Social Security Administration. 2015. 8. <http://oig.ssa.gov/sites/default/files/audit/full/pdf/A-06-14-34030_0.pdf>.

[282] Fichtner, Jason and Robert Greene. "Curbing the Surge in Year-End Federal Government Spending: Reforming "Use It or Lose It" Rules." Mercatus Center, George Mason University. September 2014. 18. <http://mercatus.org/sites/default/files/Fichtner-Year-End-Spending.pdf>.

[283] Westwood, Sarah. "Federal bureaucracies go on end-of-year spending sprees to avoid budget cuts." *Washington Examiner*. 16 July 2015. <http://www.washingtonexaminer.com/federal-bureaucracies-go-on-end-of-year-spending-sprees-to-avoid-budget-cuts/article/2563175>.

[284] Sinclair, Dean W. "Changing the Culture of Wasteful Spending in the Federal Workforce," Testimony Before the Subcommittee on Federal Spending Oversight and Emergency Management. 30 September 2015. 1. <http://www.hsgac.senate.gov/download/?id=CF8F3FC9-2EF4-467B-921E-FA9271F5C4A8>.

[285] "Memorandum Report 15-12 – Area Development Grant Applications and Approvals." Office of Inspector General of the Appalachian Regional Commission. 27 March 2015. 1. <http://www.arc.gov/images/aboutarc/members/IG/Report15-12-AreaDevelopmentGrantApplicationsAndApprovals.pdf>

[286] "ETA Needs to Improve Awarding of Year-End National Emergency Grants." Department of Labor Office of Inspector General. 30 Sep. 2015. PDF 2. <http://www.oig.dol.gov/public/reports/oa/2015/02-15-205-03-390.pdf>

[287] Tiemann, Mary and Adam Vann. "Hydraulic Fracturing and Safe Drinking Water Act Regulatory Issues." Congressional Research Service. 13 July 2015. PDF 2. <http://www.lankford.senate.gov/imo/media/doc/Hydraulic%20Fracturing%20and%20Safe%20Drinking%20Water%20Act%20Regulatory%20Issues.pdf>.

[288] Tiemann, Mary and Adam Vann. "Hydraulic Fracturing and Safe Drinking Water Act Regulatory Issues." Congressional Research Service. 13 July 2015. 14. <http://www.lankford.senate.gov/imo/media/doc/Hydraulic%20Fracturing%20and%20Safe%20Drinking%20Water%20Act%20Regulatory%20Issues.pdf>.

[289] Office of Research and Development. "Assessment of the Potential Impacts of Hydraulic Fracturing for Oil and Gas on Drinking Water Resources (external review draft)." Environmental Protection Agency. June 2015. <http://ofmpub.epa.gov/eims/eimscomm.getfile?p_download_id=523539>.

[290] "Billions of Dollars in Potentially Erroneous Education Credits Continue to be Claimed for Ineligible Students and Institutions." Treasury Inspector General for Tax Administration. Department of Treasury. 27 March 2015. PDF 2. <https://www.treasury.gov/tigta/auditreports/2015reports/201540027fr.pdf>.

[291] "Billions of Dollars in Potentially Erroneous Education Credits Continue to be Claimed for Ineligible Students and Institutions." Treasury Inspector General for Tax Administration. Department of Treasury. 27 March 2015. PDF 2. <https://www.treasury.gov/tigta/auditreports/2015reports/201540027fr.pdf>.

[292] "Billions of Dollars in Potentially Erroneous Education Credits Continue to be Claimed for Ineligible Students and Institutions." Treasury Inspector General for Tax Administration. Department of Treasury. 27 March 2015. 6. <https://www.treasury.gov/tigta/auditreports/2015reports/201540027fr.pdf>.

[293] "Billions of Dollars in Potentially Erroneous Education Credits Continue to be Claimed for Ineligible Students and Institutions." Treasury Inspector General for Tax Administration. Department of Treasury. 27 March 2015. 3. <https://www.treasury.gov/tigta/auditreports/2015reports/201540027fr.pdf>.

[294] "Billions of Dollars in Potentially Erroneous Education Credits Continue to be Claimed for Ineligible Students and Institutions." Treasury Inspector General for Tax Administration. Department of Treasury. 27 March 2015. 3. <https://www.treasury.gov/tigta/auditreports/2015reports/201540027fr.pdf>.

[295] "Billions of Dollars in Potentially Erroneous Education Credits Continue to be Claimed for Ineligible Students and Institutions." Treasury Inspector General for Tax Administration. Department of Treasury. 27 March 2015. 5. <https://www.treasury.gov/tigta/auditreports/2015reports/201540027fr.pdf>.

[296] "High Error Programs." Payment Accuracy. (2015). <https://paymentaccuracy.gov/high-priority-programs>.

[297] "Earned Income Tax Credit (EITC)." Payment Accuracy. 2015. <https://paymentaccuracy.gov/tracked/earned-income-tax-credit-eitc-2014#learnmore>.

[298] Davis, Beryl. "Improper Payments: Remaining Challenges and Strategies for Governmentwide Reduction Efforts." Government Accountability Office. 28 March 2012. 6. <http://www.gao.gov/assets/590/589681.pdf>.

[299] "Earned Income Tax Credit (EITC)." Payment Accuracy. 2015. <https://paymentaccuracy.gov/tracked/earned-income-tax-credit-eitc-2014#learnmore>.

[300] Crandall-Hollick. "The Earned Income Tax Credit (EITC): Administrative and Compliance Challenges." Congressional Research Service. 9 April 2015. 5. <http://www.lankford.senate.gov/imo/media/doc/The%20Earned%20Income%20Tax%20Credit%20Administrative%20and%20Compliance%20Challenges.pdf>.

[301] McTigue, James. "Paid Tax Return Preparers: In a Limited Study, Preparers Made Significant Errors." 8 April 2014. <http://www.gao.gov/assets/670/662356.pdf>.

[302] Holtz-Eakin, Douglas. "How the Affordable Care Act and the Employer Mandate Impacts Employers: An Overview." American Action Forum. 23 July 2014. <http://americanactionforum.org/testimony/how-the-affordable-care-act-and-the-employer-mandate-impacts-employers-an-o>.

[303] Eagan, Emily. "Primer: Employer Mandate," American Action Forum. April 2014. <http://americanactionforum.org/uploads/files/research/Employer_Mandate_Primer_Updated_April_PDF_Format.pdf>.

[304] "Cribsheet." National Federaltion of Independent Business. 12 July 2013. 2. <http://www.nfib.com/Portals/0/PDF/AllUsers/research/cribsheets/employer-mandate-penalties-nfib-cribsheet.pdf>.

[305] "Direct Federal Financial Interventions and Subsidies in Energy in Fiscal Year 2013." Energy Information Administration.12 March 2015. XV. <http://www.eia.gov/analysis/requests/subsidy/pdf/subsidy.pdf>.

[306] "Solar Market Insight Report 2013 Year in Review." Solar Energy Industry Association. March 2014. <http://www.seia.org/research-resources/solar-market-insight-report-2013-year-review>.

[307] According to the solar trade association, Solar Energy Industry Association, one megawatt of solar energy can power 164 homes. $5b/4,750MW=$1.052m/MW. $1.052m/164 homes=$6,418/home. "How many homes can be powered by 1 megawatt of solar energy?"Solar Energy Industries Association. <http://www.seia.org/about/solar-energy/solar-faq/how-many-homes-can-be-powered-1-megawatt-solar-energy>.

[308] "FAQ: What is US electricity by energy source?"Energy Information Administration. 31 March 2015. <http://www.eia.gov/tools/faqs/faq.cfm?id=427&t=3>.

[309] "Solar Energy Remarks Announcing Administration Proposals." President Jimmy Carter. 20 June 1979. <http://www.presidency.ucsb.edu/ws/?pid=32500>.

[310] "LSCMS Logistics Supply Chain Management System." Federal Emergency Management Administration. 10 Nov. 2015. < https://www.fema.gov/media-library/assets/videos/79442>.

[311] "FEMA's Logistics Supply Chain Management System May Not be Effective During a Catastrophic Disaster." Inspector General – Department of Homeland Security. Sept. 2014. <https://www.oig.dhs.gov/assets/Mgmt/2014/OIG_SLP_14-151_Sep14.pdf>.

[312] "FEMA's Logistics Supply Chain Management System May Not be Effective During a Catastrophic Disaster." Inspector General – Department of Homeland Security. Sept. 2014. <https://www.oig.dhs.gov/assets/Mgmt/2014/OIG_SLP_14-151_Sep14.pdf>.

[313] Mihm, J. Christopher. "High-Risk Series: An Update." Government Accountability Office. February 2015. 294. <http://www.gao.gov/assets/670/668415.pdf>.

[314] Holt, Mark and Mary Beth Nikitin. "Mixed-Oxide Fuel Fabrication Plant and Plutonium Disposition: Management and Policy Issues." Congressional Research Service 2 March 2015. PDF 2. <http://www.lankford.senate.gov/imo/media/doc/Mixed-Oxide%20Fuel%20Fabrication%20Plant%20and%20Plutonium%20Disposition%20Management%20and%20Policy%20Issues.pdf>.

[315] Mihm, J. Christopher. "High-Risk Series: An Update." Government Accountability Office. February 2015. 218. <http://www.gao.gov/assets/670/668415.pdf>.

[316] Mihm, J. Christopher. "High-Risk Series: An Update." Government Accountability Office. February 2015. 218. <http://www.gao.gov/assets/670/668415.pdf>.

[317] "Fiduciary Investment Advice." Department of Labor Employee Benefits Security Administration. 14 April 2015. 8. <http://www.dol.gov/ebsa/pdf/conflictsofinterestria.pdf>.

[318] "Fiduciary Investment Advice." Department of Labor Employee Benefits Security Administration. 14 April 2015. <http://www.dol.gov/ebsa/pdf/conflictsofinterestria.pdf>.

[319] Bradford, Hazel. "DOL moving forward on new fiduciary standard," Pensions & Investments. 24 August 2015. <http://www.pionline.com/article/20150824/PRINT/308249984/dol-moving-forward-on-new-fiduciary-standard>.

[320] "I-Corps: Killer Snail: An Interactive Marine Biodiversity Learning Tool." National Science Foundation. 15 June 2014. <http://nsf.gov/awardsearch/showAward?AWD_ID=1445413>.

[321] "I-Corps: Killer Snail: An Interactive Marine Biodiversity Learning Tool." National Science Foundation. 15 June 2014. <http://nsf.gov/awardsearch/showAward?AWD_ID=1445413>.
[322] "Killer Snails: Assassins of the Sea" <http://www.killersnails.com/games/killer-snails-assassins-of-the-sea>.
[323] "Small Business Innovation Research." Institute of Education Sciences. <http://ies.ed.gov/sbir/>
[324] "Ed Games Week Highlights the Emergence of Video Games in Education." Department of Education. <http://blog.ed.gov/2014/09/ed-games-week-highlights-the-emergence-of-video-games-in-education/>
[325] Deloura, Mark. "The White House Education Game Jam." The White House. 6 Oct. 2014. <https://www.whitehouse.gov/blog/2014/10/06/white-house-education-game-jam>.
[326] "Administrative Procedure Act" Report of the Senate Committee on the Judiciary. Page 199. <http://www.justice.gov/sites/default/files/jmd/legacy/2014/03/20/senaterept-752-1945.pdf>.
[327] "Cuban Assets Control Regulation." Treasury Department. 16 Jan. 2015. <https://www.federalregister.gov/articles/2015/01/16/2015-00632/cuban-assets-control-regulations>.
[328] "Cuba: Providing Support for the Cuban People." Commerce Department. 16 Jan. 2015. <https://www.federalregister.gov/articles/2015/01/16/2015-00590/cuba-providing-support-for-the-cuban-people>.
[329] "Groundbreaking for Trump International Hotel, Washington, D.C." Press Release. 23 July 2014. <https://www.trumphotelcollection.com/press/groundbreaking-for-trump-international-hotel-washington-dc>.
[330] "Guest Rooms & Suites." Trump Hotel, Washington, D.C. <https://www.trumphotelcollection.com/washington-dc/luxury-dc-accommodations.php>.
[331] "Groundbreaking for Trump International Hotel, Washington, D.C." Press Release. 23 July 2014. <https://www.trumphotelcollection.com/press/groundbreaking-for-trump-international-hotel-washington-dc>.
[332] "Tax Incentives for Preserving Historic Properties." National Park Service. <http://www.nps.gov/tps/tax-incentives.htm>.
[333] Turner, Greg. "Fenway Swings for $40M with Historic Designation." *McClatchy-Tribune Business News*. 8 Mar. 2012. <http://search.proquest.com/docview/926796682/CD5343A191BF4733PQ/2?accountid=45340>.
[334] "Lend Lease Starts Construction on Trump International hote, Washington, D.C." PR Newswire. 28 Jan. 2015. <http://www.prnewswire.com/news-releases/lend-lease-starts-construction-on-trump-international-hotel-washington-dc-300026998.html>.
[335] "Median and Average Square Feet of Floor Area in New Single-Family Houses Completed by Location." Census Bureau. <https://www.census.gov/const/C25Ann/sftotalmedavgsqft.pdf>.
[336] "Guest Rooms & Suites." Trump Hotel, Washington, D.C. <https://www.trumphotelcollection.com/washington-dc/luxury-dc-accommodations.php>.
[337] "Check Project Status." National Park Service. Project Number 30491. <http://tpsdev.cr.nps.gov/status/>.
[338] "Tax Expenditures Compendium of Background Material on Individual Provisions." Congressional Research Service. Dec. 2014. <http://www.gpo.gov/fdsys/pkg/CPRT-113SPRT91950/pdf/CPRT-113SPRT91950.pdf>.
[339] "2013 Report Card For America's Infrastructure." American Society of Civil Engineers. March 2013. 7. <http://www.infrastructurereportcard.org/a/documents/2013-Report-Card.pdf>.
[340] "2013 Status of the Nation's Highways, Bridges, and Transit: Conditions & Performance." Department of Transportation. <https://www.fhwa.dot.gov/policy/2013cpr/chap11.cfm>.
[341] "National Park Service – Fiscal Year 2016 Budget Justifications." National Park Service. 2015. ONPS-Summaries-22. <http://www.nps.gov/aboutus/upload/FY-2016-Greenbook.pdf>.
[342] Coburn, Tom. "Parked! How Congress' Misplaced Priorities Are Trashing Our National Treasures." Senator Tom Coburn, MD. Oct. 2013. 44. <http://www.landrights.org/ActionAlerts/Sen%20Coburn%20Report%20on%20NPS-Parked-1029131a.pdf>.
[343] "Search Past Grant Awards." National Park Service. <http://ncptt.nps.gov/rt66/grant-projects/>.
[344] "Resources." National Historic Route 66 Federation. <http://national66.org/resources/>.
[345] "Pay Ratio Disclosure." Federal Register. 18 Aug. 2015. <https://www.federalregister.gov/articles/2015/08/18/2015-19600/pay-ratio-disclosure>.
[346] "Pay Ratio Disclosure." Federal Register. 18 Aug. 2015. <https://www.federalregister.gov/articles/2015/08/18/2015-19600/pay-ratio-disclosure#p-1407>.
[347] "Pay Ratio Disclosure." Securities and Exchange Commission. 19 Oct. 2015. 189. <http://www.sec.gov/rules/final/2015/33-9877.pdf>.
[348] White, James R. "Identity Theft: Additional Actions Could Help IRS Combat the Large, Evolving Threat of Refund Fraud." Government Accountability Office. August 2014. 10. <http://www.gao.gov/assets/670/665368.pdf>.
[349] White, James R. "Identity Theft: Additional Actions Could Help IRS Combat the Large, Evolving Threat of Refund Fraud." Government Accountability Office. August 2014. PDF 2. <http://www.gao.gov/assets/670/665368.pdf>.

[350] White, James R. "Identity Theft: Additional Actions Could Help IRS Combat the Large, Evolving Threat of Refund Fraud." Government Accountability Office. August 2014. PDF 2. <http://www.gao.gov/assets/670/665368.pdf>.

[351] White, James R. "Identity Theft: Additional Actions Could Help IRS Combat the Large, Evolving Threat of Refund Fraud." Government Accountability Office. August 2014. PDF 2. <http://www.gao.gov/assets/670/665368.pdf>.

[352] White, James R. "Identity Theft: Additional Actions Could Help IRS Combat the Large, Evolving Threat of Refund Fraud." Government Accountability Office. August 2014. Page 13. <http://www.gao.gov/assets/670/665368.pdf>.

[353] Maurer, David. "Victims of Child Abuse: Further Actions Needed to Ensure Timely Use of Grant Funds and Assess Grantee Performance." Government Accountability Office. April 2015. 5. <http://www.gao.gov/assets/670/669909.pdf>.

[354] 42 U.S.C. §§13001b, 13013, 13022, 13023. <http://www.gpo.gov/fdsys/pkg/USCODE-2011-title42/html/USCODE-2011-title42-chap132.htm>.

[355] Maurer, David. "Victims of Child Abuse: Further Actions Needed to Ensure Timely Use of Grant Funds and Assess Grantee Performance." Government Accountability Office. April 2015. PDF 2. <http://www.gao.gov/assets/670/669909.pdf>.

[356] "Affirmatively Furthering Fair Housing." Federal Register. 16 July 2015. <http://www.gpo.gov/fdsys/pkg/FR-2015-07-16/pdf/2015-17032.pdf>.

[357] "Housing Discrimination." Department of Housing and Human Development. <http://portal.hud.gov/hudportal/HUD?src=/topics/housing_discrimination>.

[358] "Voters Say No to Government Role in Neighborhood Diversity," Rasmussen Reports. 25 June 2015. <http://www.rasmussenreports.com/public_content/politics/general_politics/june_2015/voters_say_no_to_government_role_in_neighborhood_diversity>.

[359] "Affirmatively Furthering Fair Housing." Federal Register. 16 July 2015. <http://www.gpo.gov/fdsys/pkg/FR-2015-07-16/pdf/2015-17032.pdf>.

[360] "H.R.1995 - Local Zoning and Property Rights Protection Act of 2015." Representative Paul Gosar. Introduced 23 Apr. 2015, <https://www.congress.gov/bill/114th-congress/house-bill/1995?q=%7B%22search%22%3A%5B%22%5C%22hr1995%5C%22%22%5D%7D&resultIndex=1>.

[361] Levinson, Daniel. "Actual enrollment and profitability was lower than projections made by the Consumer Operated and Oriented Plans and might affect their ability to repay loans provided under the Affordable Care Act," Department of Health and Human Services Office of Inspector General. July 2015. *ii*. <http://www.oig.hhs.gov/oas/reports/region5/51400055.pdf>.

[362] Levinson, Daniel. "Actual enrollment and profitability was lower than projections made by the Consumer Operated and Oriented Plans and might affect their ability to repay loans provided under the Affordable Care Act," Department of Health and Human Services Office of Inspector General. July 2015. *ii*. <http://www.oig.hhs.gov/oas/reports/region5/51400055.pdf>.

[363] "Obamacare into 2016 showing more signs of failure." Senate Republican Policy Committee. 20 Oct. 2015. <http://www.rpc.senate.gov/policy-papers/obamacare-into-2016-showing-more-signs-of-failure>.

[364] Goldstein, Amy. "More than half of ACA co-ops now out of insurance marketplaces," *The Washington Post*. 3 November 2015. <https://www.washingtonpost.com/national/health-science/more-than-half-of-aca-co-ops-now-out-of-insurance-marketplaces/2015/11/03/5ba95b86-824b-11e5-9afb-0c971f713d0c_story.html>.

[365] Fultonberg, Lorne. "Oklahoma Obamacare premiums see 35 percent hike," KFOR. 29 Oct. 2015. <http://kfor.com/2015/10/29/oklahoma-obamacare-premiums-see-35-percent-price-hike/>.

[366] James, Nathan, Jerome Bjelopera, Kristin Finklea, William Krouse, Lisa Sacco. "FY2016 Appropriations for the Department of Justice." Congressional Research Service. 15 April 2015. 22. <https://www.fas.org/sgp/crs/misc/R43985.pdf>.

[367] "Bulletproof Vest Partnership." Department of Justice. <http://ojp.gov/bvpbasi/>.

[368] "2016 Proposed Appropriations Language." Department of Justice. PDF 11. <http://www.justice.gov/sites/default/files/jmd/pages/attachments/2015/01/30/7._2016_appropriations_language.pdf>.

[369] Vincent, Carol Hardy. "Deferred Maintenance of Federal Land Management Agencies: FY2005-FY2014 Estimates." Congressional Research Service. 21 April 2015. PDF 2. <http://naturalresources.house.gov/uploadedfiles/deferredmaintenance.pdf>.

[370] Vincent, Carol Hardy. "Land and Water Conservation Fund: Overview, Funding History, and Issues." Congressional Research Service. June 2015. 2. <http://www.lankford.senate.gov/imo/media/doc/Land%20and%20Water%20Conservation%20Fund%20Overview%20Funding%20History%20and%20Issues.pdf>.

[371] "National Park Service Fiscal Year 2016 Budget Justification." Department of the Interior, 2015. LASA-17. <http://www.nps.gov/aboutus/upload/FY-2016-Greenbook.pdf>

[372] "National Park Service Fiscal Year 2016 Budget Justification." Department of the Interior, 2015. CONST-40. <http://www.nps.gov/aboutus/upload/FY-2016-Greenbook.pdf>
[373] "National Park Service Fiscal Year 2016 Budget Justification." Department of the Interior, 2015. CONST-48. <http://www.nps.gov/aboutus/upload/FY-2016-Greenbook.pdf>
[374] "National Park Service Fiscal Year 2016 Budget Justification." Department of the Interior, 2015. CONST-46. <http://www.nps.gov/aboutus/upload/FY-2016-Greenbook.pdf>
[375] "Federal Real Property." Government Accountability Office. 2015. <http://www.gao.gov/key_issues/federal_real_property/issue_summary>.
[376] Hatch, Garrett. "Disposal of Unneeded Federal Buildings: Legislative Proposals in the 112th Congress." Congressional Research Service. 6 Aug. 2012. PDF 2. <http://www.lankford.senate.gov/imo/media/doc/Disposal%20of%20Unneeded%20Federal%20Buildings%20Legislative%20Proposals%20in%20the%20112th%20Congress.pdf>.
[377] Hatch, Garrett. "Disposal of Unneeded Federal Buildings: Legislative Proposals in the 112th Congress." Congressional Research Service. 6 Aug. 2012. PDF 2. <http://www.lankford.senate.gov/imo/media/doc/Disposal%20of%20Unneeded%20Federal%20Buildings%20Legislative%20Proposals%20in%20the%20112th%20Congress.pdf>.
[378] Hatch, Garrett. "Disposal of Unneeded Federal Buildings: Legislative Proposals in the 112th Congress." Congressional Research Service. 6 Aug. 2012. PDF 2. <http://www.lankford.senate.gov/imo/media/doc/Disposal%20of%20Unneeded%20Federal%20Buildings%20Legislative%20Proposals%20in%20the%20112th%20Congress.pdf>.
[379] Hatch, Garrett. "Disposal of Unneeded Federal Buildings: Legislative Proposals in the 112th Congress." Congressional Research Service. 6 Aug. 2012. 1. <http://www.lankford.senate.gov/imo/media/doc/Disposal%20of%20Unneeded%20Federal%20Buildings%20Legislative%20Proposals%20in%20the%20112th%20Congress.pdf>.
[380] Wise, David. "Federal Buildings Fund: Improved Transparency and Long-Term Plan Needed to Clarify Capital Funding Priorities." Government Accountability Office. July 2012. 2. <http://www.gao.gov/assets/600/592377.pdf>.
[381] Wise, David. "Federal Real Property: Current Efforts, GAO Recommendations, and Proposed Legislation Could Address Challenges." Government Accountability Office. 16 June 2015. PDF 2. <http://www.hsgac.senate.gov/download/?id=6BA52DEB-2717-41E9-A6B6-85DBD4AF2D99>.
[382] Wise, David. "Federal Real Property: More Useful Information to Providers Could Improve the Homeless Assistance Program. Sept. 2014. 22. <http://www.gao.gov/assets/670/666259.pdf>.
[383] Wise, David. "Federal Real Property: Current Efforts, GAO Recommendations, and Proposed Legislation Could Address Challenges." Government Accountability Office. 16 June 2015. PDF 2. <http://www.hsgac.senate.gov/download/?id=6BA52DEB-2717-41E9-A6B6-85DBD4AF2D99>.
[384] Mihm, J. Christopher. "High-Risk Series: An Update." Government Accountability Office. Feb. 2015. <http://www.gao.gov/assets/670/668415.pdf>.
[385] "Browning-Ferris Industries of California, Inc., d/b/a BFI Newby Island Recyclery, and FPR-II, LLC, d/b/a Leadpoint Business Services, and Sanitary Truck Drivers and Helpers Local 350, International Brotherhood of Teamsters, Petitioner." National Labor Relations Board. 27 Aug. 2015. 21. <http://apps.nlrb.gov/link/document.aspx/09031d4581d99106>.
[386] "NLRB's Joint Employer Attack," *Wall Street Journal.* 28 Aug. 2015. <http://www.wsj.com/articles/nlrbs-joint-employer-attack-1440805826>.
[387] "Browning-Ferris Industries of California, Inc., d/b/a BFI Newby Island Recyclery, and FPR-II, LLC, d/b/a Leadpoint Business Services, and Sanitary Truck Drivers and Helpers Local 350, International Brotherhood of Teamsters, Petitioner." National Labor Relations Board. 27 Aug. 2015. 21. <http://apps.nlrb.gov/link/document.aspx/09031d4581d99106>.
[388] "Browning-Ferris Industries of California, Inc., d/b/a BFI Newby Island Recyclery, and FPR-II, LLC, d/b/a Leadpoint Business Services, and Sanitary Truck Drivers and Helpers Local 350, International Brotherhood of Teamsters, Petitioner." National Labor Relations Board. 27 Aug. 2015. 21. <http://apps.nlrb.gov/link/document.aspx/09031d4581d99106>.
[389] "USDA to Invest Up to $100 Million to Boost Infrastructure for Renewable Fuel Use, Seeking to Double Number of Higher Blend Renewable Fuel Pumps." Department of Agriculture. 10 Nov. 2015. <http://www.usda.gov/wps/portal/usda/usdamediafb?contentid=2015/05/0156.xml&printable=true&contentidonly=true>.
[390] Enoch, Daniel. "USDA Seeks to Boost Availability of E15, E85 at the Pump." Agri Pulse. 29 May 2015. <http://www.agri-pulse.com/USDA-seejs-to-boost-availability-of-E15-E85-at-the-pump-05292015.asp>.

[391] Pomerleau, Kyle and Andrew Lundeed. "The U.S. Has the Highest Corporate Income Tax Rate in the OECD." The Tax Foundation. 27 Jan. 2014. <http://taxfoundation.org/blog/us-has-highest-corporate-income-tax-rate-oecd>.
[392] Pomerleau, Kyle and Andrew Lundeed. "The U.S. Has the Highest Corporate Income Tax Rate in the OECD." The Tax Foundation. 27 Jan. 2014. <http://taxfoundation.org/blog/us-has-highest-corporate-income-tax-rate-oecd>.
[393] Matheson, Thornton, Victoria Perry, and Chandara Veung. "Territorial vs. Worldwide Corporate Taxation: Implications for Developing Countries." International Monetary Fund. Oct. 2013. 3. <https://www.imf.org/external/pubs/ft/wp/2013/wp13205.pdf>.
[394] "Buying &Selling: Cross-Border Mergers and Acquisitions and the U.S. Corporate Income Tax." Business Roundtable. 10 March 2015. *ii.* <http://businessroundtable.org/resources/buying-and-selling-cross-border-mergers-and-acquisitions-and-us-corporate-income-tax>.
[395] "Impact of the U.S. Tax Code on the Market for Corporate Control and Jobs." Majority Staff Report – Permanent Subcommittee on Investigations. 30 July 2015. <http://www.hsgac.senate.gov/download/?id=15CC6093-BC05-4007-824E-BB908928B092>.
[396] "2015 Annual Report: Additional Opportunities to Reduce Fragmentation, Overlap, and Duplication and Achieve Other Financial Benefits." Government Accountability Office. April 2015. 8. <http://www.gao.gov/assets/670/669613.pdf>.
[397] "2015 Annual Report: Additional Opportunities to Reduce Fragmentation, Overlap, and Duplication and Achieve Other Financial Benefits." Government Accountability Office. April 2015. 8. <http://www.gao.gov/assets/670/669613.pdf>.
[398] Hatch, Orin. "S. 1267 Trade Preferences Extension Act of 2015." <https://www.congress.gov/114/bills/s1267/BILLS-114s1267pcs.pdf>.
[399] "Public Law 113-159, Highway and Transportation Funding Act of 2014." <https://www.congress.gov/113/plaws/publ159/PLAW-113publ159.pdf>
[400] "Dodd-Frank Progress Report Third Quarter 2015." Davis Polk LLP. 30 Sep. 2015. 2. <http://www.davispolk.com/sites/default/files/Q32015_Dodd.Frank_.Progress.Report.pdf>.
[401] Douglas Holtz-Eakin. "The Growth Consequences of Dodd-Frank." The American Action Forum. 6 May 2015. <http://americanactionforum.org/research/the-growth-consequences-of-dodd-frank>.
[402] Adams, Robert M. and Jacob P. Gramlich. "Where Are All the New Banks? The Role of Regulatory Burden in New Charter Creation." Federal Reserve Board. 16 Dec. 2015. 1. <http://www.federalreserve.gov/econresdata/feds/2014/files/2014113pap.pdf>.
[403] Bhattarai, Abha and Catherine Ho. "Four years into Dodd-Frank, local banks say this is the year they'll feel the most impact." *The Washington Post.* 7 Feb. 2014. <https://www.washingtonpost.com/business/capitalbusiness/four-years-into-dodd-frank-local-banks-say-this-is-the-year-theyll-feel-the-most-impact/2014/02/07/12c7ca48-877e-11e3-a5bd-844629433ba3_story.html>.
[404] DeHaven, Tad. "Supplemental Security Income: A Costly and Troubled Welfare Program." CATO Institute. Aug. 2013. <http://www.downsizinggovernment.org/ssa/supplemental-security-income#_ednref>.
[405] Bertoni, Daniel. "Supplemental Security Income: Better Management Oversight Needed for Children's Benefits." Government Accountability Office. June 2012. 28. <http://www.gao.gov/assets/600/591872.pdf>.
[406] Schnepf, Randy and Brent Yacobucci. "Renewable Fuel Standard (RFS): Overview and Issues." Congressional Research Service. 14 March 2013. PDF 2. <http://www.lankford.senate.gov/imo/media/doc/2nd%20Renewable%20Fuel%20Standard%20Overview%20and%20Issues.pdf>.
[407] Schnepf, Randy and Brent Yacobucci. "Renewable Fuel Standard (RFS): Overview and Issues." Congressional Research Service. 14 March 2013. PDF 2. <http://www.lankford.senate.gov/imo/media/doc/2nd%20Renewable%20Fuel%20Standard%20Overview%20and%20Issues.pdf>.
[408] Bracmort, Kelsi. "Intermediate-Level Blends of Ethanol in Gasoline, and the Ethanol "Blend Wall."" Congressional Research Service. 1 July 2011. 5. <http://www.lankford.senate.gov/imo/media/doc/Intermediate%20Level%20Blends%20of%20Ethanol%20in%20Gasoline%20and%20the%20Ethanol%20Blend%20Wall.pdf>.
[409] Schnepf, Randy and Brent Yacobucci. "Renewable Fuel Standard (RFS): Overview and Issues." Congressional Research Service. 14 March 2013. 16. <http://www.lankford.senate.gov/imo/media/doc/2nd%20Renewable%20Fuel%20Standard%20Overview%20and%20Issues.pdf>.
[410] Salvo, Alberto and Franz Geiger. "Reduction in Local Ozone Levels in Urban Sao Paulo due to a Shift from Ethanol to Gasoline Use." Nature Geoscience. 28 April 2014. <http://www.nature.com/ngeo/journal/v7/n6/full/ngeo2144.html>.

[411] "FAQ: How much oil consumed by the United States comes from foreign sources?" Energy Information Agency. 15 Sep. 2015. <http://www.eia.gov/tools/faqs/faq.cfm?id=32&t=6>.

[412] "Affirmative Action and Non-Discrimination Obligations of Contractors and Subcontractors Regarding Individuals with Disabilities." Federal Register. 24 Sept. 2013. <http://www.gpo.gov/fdsys/pkg/FR-2013-09-24/pdf/2013-21228.pdf>.

[413] "Key Labor, Employment, and Immigration, Regulatory Initiatives in the Obama Administration." U.S. Chamber of Commerce. 13 May 2015. 14. <https://www.uschamber.com/sites/default/files/5132015_reg_issues_update_for_lrc.pdf>.

[414] McCarthy, James and Richard Lattanzio. "Ozone Air Quality Standards: EPA's 2015 Revision." Congressional Research Service. 29 Oct. 2015. PDF 2. <http://www.lankford.senate.gov/imo/media/doc/Ozone%20Air%20Quality%20Standards%20EPAs%202015%20Revision.pdf>.

[415] McCarthy, James and Richard Lattanzio. "Ozone Air Quality Standards: EPA's 2015 Revision." Congressional Research Service. 29 Oct. 2015. PDF 2. <http://www.lankford.senate.gov/imo/media/doc/Ozone%20Air%20Quality%20Standards%20EPAs%202015%20Revision.pdf>.

[416] McCarthy, James and Claudia Copeland. "Clean Air Act: A Summary of the Act and its Major Requirements." Congressional Research Service. 11 January 2013. 4. <http://www.lankford.senate.gov/imo/media/doc/Clean%20Air%20Act%20A%20Summary%20of%20the%20Act%20and%20Its%20Major%20Requirements.pdf>.

[417] "Final Audit Report: Federal Information Security Management Act Audit 2014." Office of Personnel Management. 12 Nov. 2014. <https://www.opm.gov/our-inspector-general/reports/2014/federal-information-security-management-act-audit-fy-2014-4a-ci-00-14-016.pdf>.

[418] Barrett, Devlin, Danny Yadron and Damian Paletta. "U.S. Suspects Hackers in China Breached About 4 Million People's Records, Officials Say." *The Wall Street Journal.* 5 June 2015. <http://www.wsj.com/articles/u-s-suspects-hackers-in-china-behind-government-data-breach-sources-say-1433451888>.

[419] Smith, Ian. "OPM Releases New List of FAQs on Data Breach." FedSmith. 19 June 2015. <http://blogs.fedsmith.com/2015/06/19/opm-releases-new-list-of-faqs-on-data-breach/>.

[420] Bennett, Cory. "Largest federal workers union sues OPM over breach." *The Hill.* 30 Jun. 2015. <http://thehill.com/policy/cybersecurity/246506-largest-federal-workers-union-sues-opm-over-breach>.

[421] Burr, Richard. "S.754 - Cybersecurity Information Sharing Act of 2015." Introduced 17 Mar. 2015. <https://www.congress.gov/bill/114th-congress/senate-bill/754>.

[422] Dorado, Gene. "Government Efficiency and Effectiveness: Opportunities to Reduce Fragmentation, Overlap, and Duplication and Achieve Other Financial Benefits." Government Accountability Office. 8 Apr. 2014. <http://www.gao.gov/assets/670/662366.pdf>.

[423] Farrell, Brenda. "Defense Health Care Reform: Additional Implementation Details Would Increase Transparency of DOD's Plans and Enhance Accountability." Government Accountability Office. Nov. 2013. 25. <http://www.gao.gov/assets/660/658775.pdf>.

[424] "Audit of the Department of Justice's Conference Planning and Reporting Requirements." Office of the Inspector General. Sept. 2015. *i*. <https://oig.justice.gov/reports/2015/a1531.pdf>.

Made in the USA
Middletown, DE
05 December 2016